STOP trying to prove YOU'RE right AND START proving GOD is right

EUGENE ABE

STOP TRYING TO PROVE YOU'RE RIGHT
AND START PROVING GOD IS RIGHT
Copyright © 2022 by Eugene Abe

Library of Congress Control Number: 2021924638
ISBN-13: Paperback: 978-1-64749-660-9
              ePub: 978-1-64749-661-6

Printed in the United States of America

GoTo Publish
GoToPublish LLC
1-888-337-1724
www.gotopublish.com
info@gotopublish.com

CONTENTS

WHAT'S HEAVEN LIKE?

Here's a story about a little boy
He loved to go to Grandma's and Grandpa's house
The little boy was only six years old
And he loved his Grandpa so much

He felt grandpa always had the right answers
Any time he asked him a question
So he asked grandpa if he could answer his question
His response was I'll try my best

The little boy asked him this question
How do we know, what heaven will be like
Pap, thought for a moment
Then asked the little boy to follow him

They lived in a very old house
Which didn't have a basement in it
All it had was a crawl space
A little door opened to get inside

Pap gave the little boy a flashlight
Opened the door to the little crawl space
Told the little boy to crawl into it
And asked him, what it was he saw

The little boy crawled into that crawl space
And told Pap just what he saw
Pap I see all types of crawling creatures
And spider webs hanging all around

And Pap this place is so scary
I don't want to stay here to long
For it's not a pleasant place
Pap I'm coming out right now

The little boy crawled out from under the house
And his Pap spoke gently to him
That is what hell is going to be like
Only multiplied over and over again

But Pap I asked you, what heaven would be like
Pap smiled but I had to show you this first
For hell isn't a place anyone would want to go
It's so scary you don't ever want to go there

The little boy looked up to his grandpa
I don't ever want to go there
But Pap will you answer my question,
What is heaven going to be like?

The sun had just gone down
It was starting to get real dark
Pap took him to the middle of the yard
They laid down and he told the little boy to look up

Then Pap asked the little boy by his side
Son, what is it you now see
The little boy looked up and responded to him
He was excited as to what he saw

Pap I see the big round moon
That is shining so brightly tonight
It's lighting the fields around me
Yes we can see very far

And Pap there seems to be millions of stars
Some stand out more than others
And Pap some of those stars up there
Seems to be winking at me

The sky, the fields, and all around me
Make me feel so good inside
Can we stay here the rest of the night?
This place just makes me feel good

Pap then spoke with a gentle voice
My son this is what heaven will be like
You will have a peace in your heart
An the beauty will be hard to explain

When each of us get to heaven
Then we will find Jesus there
Yes heaven will be so much better
Than anything you could comprehend on earth

The beauty you saw this very night
It's just a small glimpse of what heaven will be
So my child, always walk with Jesus
As you live your days here on earth

Yes heaven will be so much more
Than what we saw this very night
So we never want to miss a beat
We must walk with the Lord every day

So son we need to go to bed,
Tomorrow we can enjoy so much more
For everything He's provided for us
Is for each of us to enjoy

Grandson has your question been answered
Or have I failed to answer it well
The bible doesn't say a lot about heaven
Yet being with Jesus will make it even better

The grandson responded rapidly
Oh Grandpa you did so well
I can always depend on you
To answer the questions I have

Pap responded back to him
Grandma and I won't always be here
For one day the Lord will take us
To that heaven so beautiful and fair

Then you'll have to keep telling others
What you've been taught and you have learned
So don't fail the Lord in all that you do
Be found faithful each day that you live

Oh Pap I don't want you to leave me
But I know there's a time for each of us
So I'll make sure that I'll be found faithful
So we'll all meet again in heaven

    Written On: 3-24-14

SALVATION

Salvation is not a movement
Which man drummed, up
Salvation has been upon this earth
Ever since this world began

It comes to us in different ways
The first way through sacrifices
Yet it couldn't fully take away our sins
Until Jesus became the perfect sacrifice

So many believe that salvation
Is not for us today
Or they think they can put it off
Till the end of their life

Many think you get salvation
Because mom and dad belong to the church
Or because you're born in the USA
Neither one of those will work

Some believe you receive salvation
When you're baptized as a little child
You just can't pray over someone
And they receive it just like that

Others believe you receive salvation
When you're baptized as an adult
When they dunk you under the water
You then become a Child of God

Some believe you become a Christian
At the time you join the church
Yet when you join the church
You're only joining an organized body

Others believe when you're born
You automatically are a Christian
So they now can do what they want
And God will receive them into heaven

Many think if they pray the sinner's prayer
That will make them a Christian
But that is only a half truth
If you don't mean it, you're not saved

Salvation isn't any of these
Salvation was paid for on that tree
Jesus died, then He was buried
On the third day He rose again

Salvation is a free gift
Anyone can receive it, if your heart is open
But if you reach out to receive Christ
You must mean it with your whole heart

If you ask Christ into your heart
By the words in which you speak
If you don't mean it from your heart
You'll not be born again

God's only looking for serious people
Which has the desire for their life to change
From the old life to a new one
Wanting joy to flow right in

God won't receive a selfish person
That wants to straddle the fence
By believing what they want to
Giving the rest of the time to the world

God, yes, God our creator
Makes it clear to us in His word
That He is a jealous God
He wants our whole heart or nothing at all

The question each must ask yourself
Am I tired of the life I live
Is the life I'm now living
Bringing glory to the Lord Jesus Christ

The Lord can change you from the inside out
Renew your life through and through
Where you'll have a peace within
And it will not be a false pretense

When you totally commit your life to Christ
Your life will take on a desire for Him
You'll know that very moment
That you have been born again

You'll desire to tell others
Of what Christ has done for you
It will then give you a peace of mind
A peace which you've never had

Because Jesus has renewed your whole mind
You now desire what he has for you
He now becomes your dearest friend
You'll begin to share it wherever you go

Stop serving all those dead Gods
The world keeps teasing you with
Then turn your life totally over to Jesus
The one and only true God

Please don't wait another moment
Then enjoy the best for your life today
This moment surrender your all to Jesus
He'll welcome you with open arms

Written On: 11-6-13

MANY THINK

This is a very strange topic
But it needs to be addressed my friend
For it is important what we think
It is so important to God

Too often people in this world
Especially in the church today
Believe they can pick and chose
Only the things they want from God

That's why there are so many denominations
Then multitudes of churches within
And multitudes of independent churches
Stretched all around the world

Can every one of them be right?
I'm afraid every one of them has some untruth
And many are lined with untruth
How can we say, they all are right

There is only one truth we can trust
That's the Holy Word of God
Too often we find one thing in it
And we take it out of context

That thing in which we have found
Now has become so powerful to us
We never totally check the scriptures
Which will prove, we are wrong

You may say, what do you mean by that
Let's put our thinking cap on
The best way to test the truth you've found
Is to write down all scriptures people use against it

You list all the scriptures you use
Then list all the ones others use
Now you are ready to study
Whether your belief is right or wrong

Now it's time to study the whole counsel of God
How do we need to start?
We need first to go to God in prayer
That He prepares our heart to receive

We need to ask the Lord to clear our mind
Of the way we now see it
And to open our mind to receive
What the Lord will reveal to us

Even if we are proven wrong
In the thinking which we have
We'll be willing dear Lord to change
And cast aside the untruth we have

Dear Lord this applies to whatever side
Of the question I have before me
For Lord I'm only looking for truth
Not my will, but thine be accomplished

Now dear Lord as I look at this passage
Give me the setting, each passage speaks about
I'll read many passages before it
And many passages after it

If I dear Lord haven't read it
With truly an open mind
May I keep reading it over and over again
Until the passage truly jumps out to me

Lord I truly know it's the only way
I can get the true mind of God
Truly it's not my will I want
But I truly want your mind dear Lord

When we truly come to that mentality
We're now open to receive, if we're right or wrong
For God truly wants to give us truth
So our hearts can be truly blessed

But Lord, there's one thing I want
More than anything else in life
That you to be lifted up through it
And there will be less and less of me

I don't want to be puffed up
So that my life will shine
But I want you to shine through me
So heaven will be seen, not me

Now Lord my heart is now prepared
And I know your word doesn't lie
So I'm open to how it turns out
My desire is to find your will

Be assured God will reveal to you
It may be the opposite of your thinking
Or what your church or denomination has taught you
But remember it's alright, for you want God's will

It's so important to get God's will
Don't be afraid to step outside your church
And listen to many other preachers
That teaches things different than yours

Yet don't fail to be found faithful
To the church in which you attend
For your church is so important
For you to be obedient to God's word

It's through getting the thoughts of others
Then going back to the word of God
Once you have proven it totally wrong
Then ask the Lord to totally clear your mind

We'll find that much, of what we have learned
Is far from the truth of God's word
For much of what we've been taught
Is nothing more than a half truth

How can I say this, with an open mind
I can say God has changed much in me
I thought I was definitely right
When God proved to me, I was wrong

So won't you talk to the Lord, seriously?
God's word is always right
But remember the Bible was written to believers
It's confusing to the ears of the unsaved

Then remember, God's word never lies
If it lied, we wouldn't be serving the right God
So we must go to the word with this understanding
We'll stop picking and choosing, what we want to believe

Then remember the Bible is a living word
It can't be studied as other books
We must ask for the mind of Christ
That He reveals to us the truth

God will never reveal things to us
Until we stop taking praise for ourselves
And we only search the scriptures
To lift up Christ and no one else

Are you ready, to find truth
Or are you wanting to puff up yourself
If your desire is to puff up yourself
You will never find real truth

Written On: 3-19-14

NOT EVERYTHING THAT'S BAD IS BAD

A child born into this world
Yet death comes to their life
Most say what a tragedy
That God allowed it to happen

Many think that God doesn't like them
But remember God loves everyone
God thinks in a much different way
Than man does on this earth

A couple reasons God may have allowed it is,
God sees what's ahead in their life
And God takes them from this earth
Before there accountable for their sins

Others he may take life from them
Even if there a child of God
Because many may come to the Lord
By the tragedy they went through

It could be a dad or a mom
Or a friend along the way
That is drawn to the Savior
Because of the life of Christ they lived

We must learn that God always
Has a reason for what happens in our lives
It's for us to seek the Lord each day
To find out what Christ has for us

For many people God may hold blessings back
From you having many things
Or even a lot of money
For you wouldn't know how to handle it

Once you know, the Lord Jesus Christ
And you have little upon this earth
You enjoyed your life every day
Having little trouble along the way

You thanked the Lord for all you had
Even though you had very little
The smallest things you received
You appreciated, every one of them

If you had received a lot of money
Your life would have totally changed
You wouldn't have enjoyed little things in life
And all the old friends which you had

Now you're thinking of making changes
Of things you can purchase for your self
Then things would become your idol
Rather than serving the Lord Jesus Christ

The Lord holding things back from you
Is for you, a very good thing
For it keeps your eyes on Jesus
Rather than for you to serve the devil

Let's look at some which are healed
And others which are not
Does God love one better than another
Or does he have a purpose for your life

God wants us to serve him fully
Through the thick and the thin
Whether we may be healed or not
Christ needs to still be number one

It could be God doesn't heal you now
Or even your whole life in the future
For he knows you will serve him
Whether you are healed or not

But some may view there healing
As what they have done themselves
And they never give credit to God
For allowing you to be healed

Which may lead you down the wrong road
Yes a road of sin and shame
When if you hadn't been healed
You may still be serving Christ

There's another area we need to see
That deals with our Savior above
When he died, was buried, and rose again
Many say what a tragedy it was

They pointed fingers at the crowd
And the officials of that day
Saying that these officials should die
The same death that Jesus did

But remember this was all planned out
By our Lord from the beginning of time
Which was thousands of years
Before Jesus came to this earth

Our dear Lord saw though time
How wicked man on earth would be
So he planned to send his only Son
The only perfect sacrifice for our sins

All the torture Jesus went through
As they drug and tortured Him along the way
Yes on the way to Golgotha
To be killed for you and me

His death was not taken in vain
As so many on earth would think
No, Jesus's life was not taken
He allowed his life to come to an end

You may say he didn't have a choice
All odds were against our Savior
But he could have stopped them in their tracks
By calling ten thousand angles

Jesus took a look at you and me
We wouldn't have had any hope
So he chose to die that you and I
Could be set free from our sins

So he died and was buried
His enemies thought it was the end of him
But during his death he went to hell
And grabbed the keys to the bottomless pit

Then he came back and rose again
Many said it was impossible to happen
But you don't know the God I serve
The stone was rolled away, and he came forth

They had sealed the tomb, and placed a heavy stone
Which a few men could not move
Then they placed guards around the clock
For He said in three days he would rise again

If he hadn't kept his word
Of rising on the third day
We could say he wasn't God
For God always keeps his word

No, coming to Christ isn't free
As man woman and child wants to believe
For it also costs you dearly my friend
We must surrender everything to Him

No, God won't accept a portion
Of your life on earth
For if you only give Christ a portion
Satan would still have a part of you

But if you will give Christ your all
Yes surrender everything to him
Your life will totally change
To conform to the things of Him

No you don't have to give everything up
As man on earth will tell you
But once you surrender your life to Christ
Your desires will want the things of Him

So your friends, which you once had,
Which served Satan, by your side
If they don't surrender to Jesus
They will quickly flee from you

If you surrender all to Jesus
Meaning it with your whole heart
Your life will soon be surrounded
With people who truly love the Lord

Won't you surrender to Christ today
Give him your whole heart
You'll never regret the move
And God will make a place for you in heaven

So Christ going to the cross
Died and then came forth from the tomb
Wasn't a bad thing, but a good thing
So you and I, could be set free

Written On:12-22-14

COUNTERFEIT

Counterfeit is portrayed, in so many ways
It has been used throughout all times
But most do not realize
What is behind those counterfeits

Counterfeits come in many package
They're driven by Satan himself
If he can deceive you into believing in them
He has you totally in his grips

This world is full of counterfeits
There everywhere in which you turn
Satan has pulled out all the stops
In order to deceive you right into hell

Counterfeits start at the very top
Yes leaders of this world
I don't say it to make things up
It's backed by the word of God

Anything which goes against the word of God
Is a counterfeit in this world
Satan starts at the very top
Through them, he can change a whole nation

Things which we buy everywhere
Many of them are counterfeit
They have stolen from someone else
Making things which you can't tell from the original

There are things which others make
They're making it much cheaper
Yet it looks just like the original one
So they out sell the original

But as I said at the very first
That it starts at the very top
We have a counterfeit president
Running our nation, yes he is counterfeit

How do we know, he's a counterfeit president
He doesn't believe in our constitution
He's deceiving most people living here
And they accept everything he say

It's all about a one world order
No matter what our constitution says
He does what he wants to change this nation
Not caring whom he may destroy

He'll twist arms to force people to vote
For the things against our constitution
Deceiving people into believing
That everything will work out alright

He convinced the leaders to vote for
The health bill filled with thousands of pages
Saying vote for the bill to get it passed
And we'll deal with the problems later

He deceived the leaders of this nation
To pass the hate bill as quick as they could
Everyone loves doing away with hate
But that's how he deceived the people

What the hate bill was about
Was to quite the Christians around this nation
Which is totally against the constitution
The Christian, was the only one it was for

Who was behind getting this passed?
Museum's, so they could advance in this nation
They got just what they wanted
And the Christian attacks are rapidly increasing

Every time they come against a Christian
It plants fear in so many Christian's lives
So they hold back in teaching God's word
The churches have become so weak

What Christians must come to realize
The laws of God, supersede the laws of man
And if we don't follow God's Holy Word
We will be sent straight to hell

We have a ruthless enemy
Which is out to destroy our lives
He already knows his destination is hell
He wants to drag everyone to hell with him

So many are falling for his tactics
Yes Christians which have surrendered to Christ
There following him one step at a time
Being deceived by the enemy of their soul

Yet the Savior of our soul
Has made a hiding place for each of us
When we truly accept Christ into our heart
We can hide in the arms of God

Yet we still can't let our guard down
For Satan will deceive you in any way he can
Won't you stay close to the Savior's side
Asking the Holy Spirit to lead the way

Yield to the Holy Spirit each step of the way
Don't push His gentle tugging away
For if we give Satan one inch of our life
He'll never stop there my friend

He'll send little things, past your life each day
Things which really doesn't seem bad
Many times they are only things
Consuming your time, so you don't have time for Christ

Time to daily read your bible
Yet it multiplies as the days pass by
So you'll never think anything about it
Until Satan has total control of your life

It starts out so innocently
Then it multiplies as the days go by
So you'll never think anything about it
Until Satan has your total life

Don't think one minute that Satan
Can't snatch you out of the arms of Jesus
Yes Jesus will hold onto us tightly
Yet we ourselves can cast ourselves out

Many get so caught up in their kids
Their minds each day is consume with them
They drown the voice of the Savior out
Without considering that it's an attack of Satan

So it's important to set aside time each day
To get alone with the Savior above
So He can speak to your heart
Along with you, bringing to Him your every cares

Be assured Christ will never leave you
But you can, if you don't keep that bond
With Christ each day that you live
Won't you stay close to the cross

Yes, people may make fun of you
But remember God said we would be
A peculiar people which serve him
You may say, what does peculiar mean

It means you are set apart
From the ways of this old world
Totally focused on Jesus
The Savior of our soul

We're not a bunch of weird people
With no one directing our path
But a person which gives Christ all of our life
Spreading the love of God wherever we go

We don't cave into peer pressures
For, they will lead you down the wrong road
The road designed for Satan and his angels
You surely don't want to go there

Just the smile we carry on our face
Will bring joy to others we meet
Then they will hunger for what we have
They'll open the door, by asking us questions

No, Christians shouldn't carry a sad face
It shows you don't enjoy your life
Many think they have to be long faced
In order to get to the Lord

Yet God above wants all of us
Which have surrendered our heart to Him
To be the happiest people on earth
So they can see why serving Jesus, is the best

Many say they don't like, those does and don'ts
But there's a good reason for them
God's not holding a hammer over our head
To punish us every time we make a mistake

But He gave us laws to live by
Not just to punish us for our wrongs
His laws are designed to keep us on track
The pathway that leads us to heaven

Won't you get on board with Christ
And stop being that counterfeit Christian
For counterfeit Christians won't make it to heaven
For they are serving Satan instead of the Lord

So get on board by committing your life to Christ
With no reservation in your heart
Turn from the old life that you lived
Serve the Lord with everything within you

Time is running out for you my friend
Most signs of Christ's return, have all been fulfilled
The next sign which will take place
Is the rapture of the Church

Those which are totally surrendered to Christ
Keeping their lives cleansed from sin
Making themselves ready when Christ returns
He will come as a thief in the night

Then if your life is not prepared
Trying to stay to close to the edge
Be assured you will be left behind
That's what Satan wants to happen to you

So don't worry if man should make fun of you
It will only be for a little while
Compared to eternity being with Jesus
What a blessed day it will be for the redeemed

But for you which are wanting to play around
Thinking one day I'll come to the Lord
Be assured most will not have enough oil
And you'll live eternity in the pit of hell

Today is the day of salvation
We're not guaranteed another chance
Won't you make your choice to surrender to Jesus
So your eternity will be with the Lord

Written On: 8-27-15

GOD GAVE US ALL A WILL

From the very beginning of time
God didn't want us to be a puppet
As the angels in heaven
They are constantly worshiping the Lord

Yet our God up in heaven
After creating the earth and all in it
Yes, He created the earth, water, and land
The heavens, and then He created man

Now after Adam named all the animals
God saw that something was missing
All the animals had a mate
In order to replenish the earth

Adam was all alone
With no one to commune with
So God put Adam to sleep
Took one of his ribs, and made woman

Yes this shows how man is to be the leader
Of the world in which we live
Yet not to be a dominate person
Over the mate He gave to him

God placed them in the garden
In order for them to work together
Not to take advantage of each other
That their lives could marvelously be blessed

God saw that when each work together
A great bonding would take place
Then at the same time
He didn't want them to be as the angels in heaven

So He gave them a choice to make
By telling them they could eat from every tree
But the one placed in the middle of the garden
Yes the tree called good and evil

Now the Lord stepped back and waited
To see if Adam would make the right choice
Yet, the woman which God made from Adam's rib
Allowed the serpent to deceive her

Then she proceeded to convince Adam
That it was alright to partake of it
Adam should have rejected it
Since he was the leader of the family

So he was thrown out of the garden
Yes the garden a perfect place
All because Adam made the wrong choice
He set the pace for you and me

But it's up to you and I to decide
What will I do with my life
From this time forward
Every one of us have a will

We can blame it all on Adam
But that does no good for us
That's what Satan wants to happen
He loves you playing the blame game

For as long as were blaming others
We'll never see where we've gone wrong
So as long as you stay right there
Your life will continue getting worse

That's how Satan will deceive you
By telling you to continue blaming
There seems to be no way
For you to ever change your life

While the Lord is saying unto you
I gave you a will to choose
So you can decide the type of life
Which you will live today

Your choice is the same choice
He gave Adam and Eve in the garden
So, stop blaming how you're living your life
On Adam and Eve in the beginning

Start living your life each day
To please the Lord up in heaven
The Lord knows what's best for us
Stop trying to live your life for self

The choice is in your hands
Will you serve, the Lord above
Or will you serve the god of self
So your life will end up in hell

Always remember, the Lord knows what's best
For every one of us on earth
That's why He gave us His Holy Word
So, we will have direction for our life

His direction never changes
He's been the same since the very beginning
It's man that tries to change the Word
Yet it's still the same, whether man changes it or not

What is meant by that?
You can change it all you want
Yet God will still judge us
By his original word

That's why God gives us direction
That we would always know how to live
Not like all the gods of this earth
Which constantly change with the times

For they've caved into political correctness
So you never know what's really expected
But that's where Satan wants you to be
For it keeps your mind off of Christ

God will never force you to serve Him
For He wants you to make your own choice
In the direction which you will live
Will it be for God, or will it be for the devil

The best choice anyone can make
Is surrender your whole life to Christ
Then live for Christ every day
You can then be assured of heaven

Written On: On: 2-3-15

A PARABLE OF THE LAWN MOWER

As I stand back and watch people
Mow their lawns each and every week
Some of the lawns look real good
Others you can say, they've been mowed

Each thought they took pride in their lawn
Yet there was a great difference in each
As each took pride as they mowed there lawn
What makes each of them difference

Well it is the type of mower you use
The quality of the mower makes a difference
Of how the lawns will turn out
Let's take a closer look at them

I'll use myself as an example
So the same operator is using it
For the one that's using the mower
Makes a big difference of the job when finished

At the beginning of my business
I always took pride in the work I did
I was talked into buying a Cub Cadet
Walk behind mower, which was forty eight inches

I wasn't allowed on the front of the lawns
Because of the terrible job which it did
For it made so many streaks on it
I had to mow the front lawn with a small mower

The big mower would cut into the ground
If you were mowing on a slop
And the other side of the mower
Left the lawn, quit high

Several years later I bought
An expensive mower, the same size
The people still wouldn't let me use it
They remembered the bad job the other had done

But that year we got so much rain
The lawn was growing too fast
To keep up with the little mower
So I told them I had to use the big walk behind

I've been using the mower ever since
They were proud of the job they saw
Now what was the big difference in each
Which gave the super job, compared to the other

The difference was a floating deck
Along with it having many more RPM's
Which sucked the grass in a standing position
The grass was all cut the same

The big and expensive mower
Run so very much smoothly
Yes the parts cost so much more
Yet they worked for multiple times longer

Few people never weigh the cost
When they go out to buy a mower
There only looking at the mower
And they fail to count the cost

When you buy five more mowers
In the same time that expensive one was bought
Now it costs you so much more than if you had
Bought the expensive one in the first place

Now stop, that's not all of the savings
The down time rarely happens
So you're not running all over town
Spending gas and time to get the job done

These are costly things my friend
We must take into consideration
And consider the much more beautiful job
Which the more expensive mower does

Then people fail to think about
All the pressures the cheap one causes
Now you end up with an ulcer
For all the worrying you have done

Satan wants us to see surface things
Not to ever look at all phases which may come
He knows if you annualize all things
You would buy the better one, to have less stress

God wants us to totally love Him
By serving Christ everyday
Giving Him first place in your life
And stop giving Him second best

The Lord wants, what's best for us
He can only give it, if were seeking Him
Rather than what we want
Because we want our own way

Be assured if you seek your will
Rather than seek the will of the Lord
There are very rough roads you will face
You won't have Christ to lead the way

Just as that cheap or inexpensive lawn mower
It may give you a decent job for a while
But before long it will start breaking down
And you can't handle all the stress

Stress is so terrible to go through in life
It will break down your health day by day
Before long, you'll have bigger problems
All because you didn't let Christ lead the way

You give into peer pressures
The world keeps pouring into your life
Instead of turning it over to Jesus
The author and finisher of our faith

Those boo boos we do to our lawns
With those cheap lawn mowers we buy
Was there because the lawn mower I bought
Was designed with a fixed deck

So when you mow uneven lawns
Many times you cut into the ground
Now your lawn just doesn't look nice
For all the neighbors to see everyday

That reminds me of people,
Which call themselves a Christian,
Their Christianity is only lip service
For their life doesn't measure up

But we as a true Christ follower
Must live among these type people
Yet God will reveal those unto us
They're only deceiving themselves

The bible is so plain to us my friend
We have to live among these type people
But we're not to cave into their ways
For they're sending themselves to hell

But God's word shouts out to everyone
Come out from among the world
Give your life totally to me
I can help you along the way

You may have bad things come your way
But I'll be with you, as you face each test
If you continue to stay focused on me
You'll turn out alright in the end

Many of the trials you wouldn't have to go through
If you would read my word everyday
Asking me to reveal to you things
That will help you to live the right way

And spend much time talking to me
Letting me know what you're going through
What is on your mind
That you would have for me to do

Yes I know what you're going through
Yet I'll never interfere in your life
For I'm waiting for an invitation
To help you through the problems you face"

That's when you'll become, as the expensive mower,
Things in your life will start running smoothly
And that's when your life will start shining
Everywhere for all the world to see

You'll start making an impact around you
For the world will want what you have
As you live for Jesus everyday
Self will take a back step, in your life

Yes the world is looking for someone
That will step up to the plate
The sad thing is, most of us Christians
We're not living what Christ requires of us

If we continue living below the standards
Which God, has set for our life
We may find ourselves on the outside
And eventually we could miss heaven

When God says we're to be a shining light
Standing on a hill
It doesn't mean we're to be shy
By keeping the gospel to ourselves

Were to share the good news wherever we go
Exposing Jesus to the world everyday
Stop trying to smooth coat the gospel
But give others what they need to receive

Just as the expensive lawn mower
Has such torque to its mowing
It draws the grass to a standing position
And cuts the grass off very even

We as believers that share the gospel
Without the favor of men
People will start standing up and listening
To what the bible has for them

The world's not interested in what we think
Yet they will see the Lord through our actions
Our life will then reach out wider
Many more will get excited about Christ

That's when we'll grow much stronger
To take the message around the world
For our life of self, will fade away
And we'll desire to let Christ shine through us

We'll spread the gospel wherever we go
We'll spread the good news why Jesus came
He died for everyone on this earth
So you and I could be set free

Yes accepting Jesus is a free gift
But excepting Christ, it costs us our all
We must turn one hundred percent
Away from the life we once lived

Once you've used a quality lawn mower
You'll never want a cheap one again
Seeing all the benefits it has for you
Will excite you so much more

That's exactly what Christ will do for you
If you totally surrender all to Him
You'll not want to turn back to the world
For there's nothing for us to embrace

But if you should falter along the way
As a mower will break down
You'll quickly go to the Cross and repent
And be assured, he'll be waiting for you

He'll forgive your past you have done
Never to remember them anymore
If you are the one to bring it up, remember,
Christ doesn't want you to hold onto it

He's placed it under the blood
When He went to Calvary's hill
Died, was buried, and rose again
So you and I could be set free

Why put it off another moment
Christ is waiting for you to repent
So that you and I can be with him
When our life on earth is complete

Repentance is the first step
Yes repentance is free
But the next step of the verse
Is an action on our part

It says we must turn from our old ways
Taking on the Armor of God
No longer embracing the world
But embracing the Lord Jesus Christ

Are you prepared to serve the Lord
Or just to become a lukewarm person
If that is your intention
God said He would spew you out

The choice is now in your hands
Won't you make the right choice today
So the Lord will be well pleased with you
As you live your life on earth

Written On: 5-7-14

ARE YOU WILLING TO STAND ALONE

The Lord woke me up this morning
Spoke very firmly to my heart
He wanted to give me a message
To stir me from deep within my soul

He showed me something amazing
I pray it never happens to me
For I could be lost for eternity
Won't we take this serious my Friend

He showed me a very disturbing story
And it shocked me oh so much
I needed to put it down on paper
Before it passed from my mind

I saw four soldiers marching down
Through a town they lived in
Three were only in their civilian clothes
The one was fully dressed for battle

What disturbed me oh so much
They all marched down through the town
Never ever to look aside
Their goal was to get to the battle

People were peeping out their windows
At the very sight they saw
For these men were all up in years
But the fight was still in them

Many months had gone by
And the battle finally came to an end
It was time to go back home
To rest for a little while

The bus pulled up in the town
And the door of the bus opened
Only one of the men got off the bus
Guess who that one was

It was the soldier which was fully dressed
To go off to war, when he left months earlier
He was the only one that came back home
And he was up in years

You see he had been faithful in being prepared
For any battle that came before him
So he kept his armor close by his side
Ready to face any storm that would come

He was welcomed back home
With open arms by everyone in the town
For he had gone in their place
While they sat back and relaxed

Then the Lord showed me another picture
Yes it flashed before my very eyes
Of people not ready for battle
That live all across the world

He showed me multitudes of people
Who say they love the Lord
Yet they have failed to put there armor on
They love dabbling with the things of the world

Yes they say that they're in the battle
But their life doesn't measure up
To what the bible has taught them
Even though they say they love Him so

They say they have their armor on
They've repented of their sins
But the fruit which they're bearing
Can't be seen by any around them

Yes they had lived their lives for many years
For the Lord had made an impact in them
They had shared the Lord before many people
But in their later years had given up

Their attitude was to let the young take over
When the Lord had prepared them for this very hour
The wisdom they had for the next generation
Was a powerful message to all the world

But they left their lives burn out
For they had taken on to big a task
Yes they were trying to do every thing
To every man and woman on earth

But they failed to do what the Lord
Had placed before them to do
Yes God has something for all to do
He tells us to stay in His perfect will

One servant was only given one talent
One he gave five, the other ten
He knew what each one could handle
That's why everyone in the church is different

Each has different jobs to do
For the Lord knows what you can handle
He'll not give you any more than you can handle
There's a question each must ask himself

Have I been faithful to the task before me?
Yes the task God has for me to do,
Or am I fooling around with my salvation?
Don't let Satan mess with your mind

He's a deceiver and he's a liar
He'll cause you to miss heaven
If you allow him to mess with your mind
The question is, what will I decide?

How can I keep Satan, out of my life
I'll give you a couple ways
Which will help you keep on track
Don't mess around with the things of this world

What are you doing this very hour?
To help you stay on track my friend
You need to set a special time each day
To read and study God's Holy Word

Prepare your heart to receive the things
God wants to help you live by
Ask the Lord to keep your heart pure
In order for you to know His will for your life

Ask the Lord to open your mind
So Satan can't enter, and block Christ out
Receiving the things which will help you
Then as He gives to you, put it in action

Also set a certain time each day
To talk to the Lord above
Then take some time to listen
For Christ to speak to your heart

Yes the Holy Spirit will talk to you
By ministering, through nudging your heart
Many times He will minister to you
By causing your mind to think about Him

He'll also speak through ministers and prophets
Yes at the time you need to hear the right thing
Once He speaks to your heart
Then follow what He tells you to do

Surround yourself with strong Christians
Ask them to help you stay on track
Be willing to take their advice
For they have your best at heart

Then find a church and be faithful
Don't keep missing, when you want to
But be faithful to each service
It will help build, your life up

The reason you do all these things
Is to not let Satan have a chance
To destroy your mind, then your soul
God will always have your best at heart

It will prepare you for that time
You may have to stand alone
For friends sometimes will deceive you
But when you're strong, you can detect it

Then you'll be able to stand alone
Depending fully on the Lord
For when you learn to trust totally in God
Christ will cover you with his blood

Anytime Satan comes snooping around
Ask the Lord to cover you with His blood
And the blood will cause him to flee away
The blood puts a wall up, between you and him

How about it my precious friend
The choice is in your hands
To whom will you trust your life?
Satan, or the Lord Jesus Christ

Written On: 3-7-15

THE MOST POWERFUL TEACHING I'VE LEARNT

Won't you listen very intently?
As I write this little message
It's something which has changed my life
Yes this truth has changed my whole thinking

Every church and denomination
Has good points and also bad
The problem with most of their thinking is
They say, you cannot change their mind

Believe me I was that very person
Where principles, were planted in my mind
And bless God you will not change me
For I know what the bible says

Yet all too often the things I'd been taught
May have been all or partially right
They had been planted in me since I was a child
And bless God no one can prove me wrong

Many of the things I learnt, was right
Yet the attitude which I had presented
That drove people farther from the Lord
Many never to enter the church again

Then those which were out in the world
When they heard how I came across to them
It drove them farther from the cross
Rather than draw them closer to the Lord

Attitude is the number one thing
You draw more people with honey than vinegar
Meaning that when we speak softly to people

They will take time to hear you out
But harsh words which are spoken
By those which call themselves Christians
Causes those of the world to flee us
Rather than draw them closer to the cross

Christian's aren't to be pushy people
Jesus set the example for us to live by
There is a big difference in being firm
As long as it flows out of a heart of love

The bible teaches us that love
Covers a multitude of sins
Meaning were never to be arrogant
When we speak to those around us

Many have been a student of the word
Thinking they could beat people over the head
Yet many of the older people of the past
Drove people farther from the cross

Bless God my denomination has taught me
For years, so I know they're right
So I'll follow my denomination
And I know that I'll make it to heaven

Don't get me wrong, I believe in denominations
Yet we're to definitely check them out
By checking out what their teaching
With the bible, God's Holy Word

Why do you think so many leave their church?
It's because many get things in their minds
Leaving the church they attended
"I'll just leave if you don't embrace me"

So they leave with bitterness in their heart
But be assured God can't bless them
For bitterness is a sin
And bitterness can't enter heaven

The bible is a book to be read
With an open mind before the Lord
To be fit together as a puzzle
Not forcing any piece together in the wrong way

For when we try forcing the wrong pieces
In a place it's not intended to go
It will cause friction in your life and the church
To never find real peace in your soul

When each piece is fit properly together
Because you have surrendered all to Christ
"When Not my will, but thy will be done"
Is all I'll except for my life

That's when your life will totally change
To be like Jesus every day
An people will long for what you have
For they see Jesus in the life which you live

I thought I was right for many years
But people didn't except what I taught
For bless God I was showing two sides
Of what a Christian was supposed to look like

God took me to many a wood shed
To get me to where I am today
He now knows that he can trust me
To change areas I need to change

He could have dumped it all on me
But He knew I couldn't process it all at once
He gave unto me, as my heart was prepared
To receive what he had for me

I've come to that place in my life dear friend
That I know whole denominations can be wrong
So I've determined to check all things out
To prove whether they're right or wrong

Believe me much of what he has taught me
Went against what I'd been taught in the past
Many were a hard pill to swallow
For they were so embedded in my soul

One day I got serious before the Lord
Saying Lord I give totally up
In the ways I've been taught throughout life
I just surrender my whole life to you

Yes I got saved at the age of seventeen
Advanced in the Lord each year that I lived
But satisfaction had never come to my soul
So God took me to many a woodshed

Then one night God began speaking to me
I was now in my sixty some years
God began speaking to my tender soul
I said Lord, I surrender all to you

I surrender all of my past thinking
Won't you change my life through and through
That's when God gave me a truth
I never ever want to forget

This truth has totally changed my life
Know longer to think as I used to think
He's changed me as how I look at His word
Which most people still think as they want

Most people when studying God's word
On a subject they want to study
They find all the passages they can find
To prove what they think is right

God spoke to me through a dream
Yes He spoke gently to my soul
I'll give you a truth to not forget
And you'll be on the right road to heaven

This is what the truth is
Stop trying to prove that you are right
But look at the scripture as man should look
Look at it to prove that God is right

When God showed me this powerful truth
I started looking at all types of subjects
Finding that much of what was being taught
Is only a half-truth, being taught as truth

I know longer take man's word as truth
I check them out, yes preacher's in the pulpit
Man is preaching nothing but half-truth
Leading people straight to the pit of hell

So how should you look at each subject
Check out all scriptures, which each say their right
Then ask the Holy Spirit to fill the gap in between
Which you're missing to connect them together

If you get serious before the Lord
Not caring, if you have to change
You'll find that so much you've been taught
Is not what God intended for your life

So, it's time to get serious before the Lord
Allowing the Lord to direct your life
Rather than following what you've believed
For most of the life in which you have lived

Written On: 10-9-15

A MIGHTY WALL

Satan is very clever
He causes us to put walls up
Most walls we have in our lives
Were so blinded we don't know they are there

We can see the walls in others
But when it comes to walls of our own
We can't see the wall we have
Because Satan has blinded our eyes

I see it happen all too often
When we deal with tender hearts
In are children which we see each week
Which are not of our own family

Most times we are having problems
With our very own children
So we think every other child
Is worse than the child we raised

You failed to raise your own child
In the love of Jesus Christ
So you look at other children
With the hate that lives in you

Oh you say that hate is not there
Yet your actions are showing through
Inside your heart buried deeply
Satan has blinded you to see

You think that other people's children
Are not good within themselves
So when you approach most children
You're always sending jabs from your lips

My eyes and ears are open
When I hear or see things like that
To the tender hearts of children
Yes, this is the perfect molding time

When we give them an eagle eye
Or speak harshly to that child
What we're saying to that tender heart
I've got my eye focused on you

And if you make the wrong move
I'll bounce on you very quickly
That child then takes an offense to you
Then they don't come back to church

You could have handled it much differently
By saying kindly, how may I help you
To make the church more enticing
You could have grabbed the heart of the child

So many, especially older people
Are set in their ways down to the core
Saying, bless God I'm proud of my life
Nobody else will tell me how to live"

We're losing a whole generation
Of children which have left the home
Which have been brought up in the church
They won't have any part of Christ, once they leave

It was reported just recently
That ninety percent never serve the Lord
They embrace the ways of the world
They won't have any part of your God

Why do they do such a thing?
Because you tell them you love the Lord
Yet the way in which you treat others
Tells them you don't love, the God you serve

So, if your God doesn't flow through you
You are not serving the God you say you serve
And if I should miss heaven
I'm sure you'll miss heaven to

Have you sent more people from the Lord
Then to point them to the cross
The question we must ask ourselves
What type impact am I making

If the church isn't growing
Maybe I could be the one
Which is hindering the work of God
In the church in which I attend

I need to go to God and ask Him
To forgive me of my past
And then I need to go to the people
The ones I've caused to stumble along the way

Asking them to forgive me of the wrongs
I've done to each of them
Some will accept your forgiveness
For the wrongs you've done to them

Others will not accept your forgiveness
It's a real shame on their part
You won't have to worry about it any more
You've now done all that you can do

God will now release you of that burden
Which you've been carrying so long
Now that you have been set free
Don't go back to the ways of your past

The past things which you used to embrace
You surrendered them all to the Lord
Then ask the Lord to direct you
In the path which you should go

As you read God's word each day
Ask the Holy Spirit to reveal to you
What he has for you to learn today
As He reveals it, you'll be willing to change

Yes, apply the truth he has given you
You'll find life is so much better
And you'll learn to love all people
No matter how bad they are

No, you don't embrace the ways of others
Yet you love the person so much
You'll share with them the love of Jesus
As Christ flows out through your life

There's so much power in the name of Jesus
If we love Jesus from deep in our soul
Our lives will become power packed
It will flow out through the life we live

Stop trying to push your beliefs on others
Embrace others in the name of Jesus
Yielding to what God has for you to do
Forgetting, what we thought was always right

Too often the things taught in the past
Don't measure up to God's Holy Word
Stop living your life for self and others
Start living your life for the Lord Jesus Christ

Then the new life in Christ you've taken on
Will make an impact wherever you go
And the Lord will be well pleased with you
As you embrace others to serve the Lord

Written On: 11-4-13

A MIRACLE

When we think of miracles
It starts our mind flowing
Thinking of all the miracles we know
That have happened to each of us

Most of the things we call miracles
Aren't miracles at all
For the dictionary tells us
A miracle is something supper natural

We will make the statement
I received a miracle today
But when you put them to the test
It wasn't a miracle at all

You received a check in the mail
On a day you needed it so much
So you called it a miracle, and you said
You didn't know where your miracle had come from

Now you put it to a test
A few weeks earlier you filed your taxes
So you knew the money was coming
It just happened to come that very day

So we couldn't call it a miracle
But something God had provided for you
For you worked and paid your taxes
You had just, over paid them too much

Now let's look at another angle
Say you knew your check was due
You knew how much you were going to receive
An the check came that very day

When you opened the envelope
You got so excited at what you saw
For the check from the IRS
Was a thousand dollars more than expected

They said they owed you money
For something you hadn't claimed
You would never have received it
If the IRS hadn't caught it

You would have filed your taxes in the drawer
Never to look at it again
Unless you were audited
By the good old IRS

So that could have been considered
In the category of a miracle
And you had every reason to get excited
You could now call it a miracle

What about a sickness you have
You take medicine from the doctor
It's proven to take care of it
If you take the full dose of the pills

When you received the healing
You can't call it a miracle
That's because God had allowed doctors
To have wisdom to give you the right pill

Now let's say you have cancer
The doctors have done all they can do
They say it's only a matter of time
Which you are going to live

The doctor doesn't have the last word
It was the Lord that gave you the first breath
Now it was up to the Lord
To give unto you the last breath

Someone came to visit you
They prayed Jesus heal this child
You were so weak and frail, but they prayed
In the name of Jesus rise up and walk

They start seeing color come back into your face
You started feeling strength come back to you
You now sit up in bed
Then you scoot over to the edge

Once your legs dropped over the edge
You forced yourself to your feet
The first thing you said to every one
Praise the Lord I am healed

That is a great miracle
No one can deny
For the doctors had given up
And in Jesus Name you sprang forth

Miracles come in different packages
Yet each one must be super natural
Now you can look back over your life
You now see very few miracles

But there is another miracle
Which people don't think of it, as one
It's the miracle of salvation
Which totally renews your life

The past sins you had in your life
They are all forgiven, never to return again
For when Christ wipes them away
He no longer can remember them any more

Yes your old life has now passed away
You have totally been renewed
So you take on the new life
You received it in Jesus name

God changes your old desires
Which you used to please yourself
To desiring to tell every one
That Jesus now lives deep within

Others see that great difference in you
Many others will come to Christ
Because you're no longer ashamed of Jesus
He's now become your dearest friend

If you've never excepted Christ into your heart
Won't you ask Christ to come in today
So you can have the greatest miracle
That Jesus provides to whosoever will

All it takes is a step of faith
Putting your trust in the Savior above
Believing it with your whole heart
And be assured Jesus will not turn you away

Written On: 3-27-14

THERE'S POWER IN THE BLOOD

The powerful force of the blood
Yes, the blood in each of our veins
Has more power than we can comprehend
It's the blood that keeps us alive

Just allow the blood drain from your veins
Through an accident of some kind
And as the blood gushes from your veins
You get weaker as each moment passes by

But if someone comes along my friend
And stops the bleeding of that wound
To stop the blood from flowing
It gave you time to get to the hospital

Then as they give you more blood
You begin to perk up again
For the blood gives us life
It's like you've been born-again

But there's another blood more powerful
The blood of Jesus sets men free
That's why Jesus went to Calvary
So whosoever will, can be set free

No, when Jesus went to that old rugged cross
It wasn't a tragedy my friend
For Jesus went to that cross willingly
He could have stopped it at any time

By calling ten thousand angles
To rescue Him from that cross
Man could never have stopped Him
Yet, He chose to follow through with it

By completing that great sacrifice
Willing that no one would perish
He went down to the pit of hell
Grabbing the keys to the bottomless pit

Where Satan will be bound for eternity
When this life comes to an end
Man will no longer be tormented
For a child of God has been set free

Jesus blood that he shed at Calvary
Was so powerful that all could be free
But we must choose to go to the Cross
So Jesus can wipe away all our sins

It is Jesus blood which He shed at Calvary
That made it available for each of us
But we must accept Christ into our heart
So that we can be born-again

It's his blood which sets us free
Yes He'll wipe away all our past sins
Never to remember them again
What a great sacrifice, He made for you and me

So won't you come to that Old Rugged Cross?
To be set free from all your sins
So you can have a joyous here after
With Jesus, for all eternity

Written On: 10-18-15

I WANT MY WILL

As each of us live our lives
How do you approach everything?
Are you one which has embraces the world
Seeking everything for yourself?

This is how Satan wants us
To live our lives everyday
And he's doing a good job at it
Just reflect back over the life you've lived

You might say, it doesn't happen to me
Yet you're only fooling yourself
For it happens to every one of us
Most don't realize what is happening

Most forget, Satan is a deceiver
He'll attack any way he can
He's always looking for a way to attack
Yes in a way which you are not expecting

Just think of those on a ball team
They want to win the game at any costs
So you pray that the Lord be by your side
To win the game in which you're playing

But there's someone on the other team
Which is praying the same prayer as you
So the Lord now has a choice to make
Just which prayer will He answer

The prayer, each should have prayed
That each team would do their best
For the one which does their best
Will be the one to come out on top

In which way, the game turns out
You will rejoice over the results
For you are determined to do your best
With respect for everyone else

You want the Lord to receive the glory
For each to do their very best
But no, after the game is over
You hold bitterness in your heart

The reason is, you didn't get your way
An your heart, is so broken
Satan has control of your life
It shows through bitterness in your heart

As a little child, that's where it starts
You've watched your mom and your dad
Possibly your brother or sister
Or some friend in your neighborhood

You start out imitating them
Then it gets embedded in your soul
So you start wanting your way
No matter who it might hurt

Everyone has taught you
At that molding time of your life
That everything you accomplish in life
Comes by wanting your own will

If that attitude isn't broken
It causes great problems throughout your life
Then when you don't get your way
You harbor bitterness in your heart

When you get to those teenage years
Your demands get so much stronger
Demanding that your parents provide
All you want for your life

The problem is, when you get things that way
You never learn to appreciate them
The demands keep getting stronger
As you receive each thing given you

When God says, "If you don't work
Then you shouldn't be able to eat"
For when you work for the things you get
You'll start appreciating the things you have

That's why so many are on welfare
It has become a generation thing
For we are teaching everyone
Don't work, for the government will provide

Most which get things that way
End up with drinking and drugs
And things which doesn't help them
But hinders them through their life

They end up with that attitude
You owe me everything I want
They end up with all those benefits
They receive more than most that work

But what they fail to realize
Sometime down the road
That money will soon run out
And what a mess you'll then be in

When God says we need to work
For the things we need in life
It's not a punishment for us
It will help us feel good about ourselves

God knows that idle hands
Will take us to places we shouldn't go
And most of the places it takes us
Is a place, headed straight to Hell

Yes idle hands lead to Satan's playhouse
To things which at first look good
But the more he gets you in his grips
He'll end up destroying your life

Satan cares nothing about you
He just wants to destroy your life
Sending you to the pit of hell
He'll finally accomplish what he set out for

But the child of God which loves
The Lord with their whole heart
When Christ tugs at their hearts door
They quickly repent and change directions

To conform into the likeness of God
So when death or the rapture takes place
Their life will be ready to
Be embraced by the Lord Jesus Christ

Yes they want to have a great eternity
With the Savior who loves us so
Knowing that they have built there treasures
In heavenly things, rather than for themselves

For they know that their life here on earth
Is short compared to eternity
So when troubles and trials come their way
They still keep focused on Christ

Self is a power force in our lives
Satan wants you to focus on it
He knows for some he doesn't have to
Send bad things to come to your life

He knows he can have Hell filled with
Good people which everyone loves
For their focus is on things of this world
And good things they can do for others

But the problem is they have been
Caught up in all those things
But they don't have time for Christ
Which is who we need to be focused on

Then because of our neglect for Jesus
When we face God on judgment day
He'll have to turn his back on us
Because of our choices on this earth

He won't be able to find the day you repented
Giving your total life to Christ
Where you turned from your past ways
Leaning on Christ to lead the way

It won't be Christ which sent you to hell
But yourself, which made the wrong choices
Be assured if you don't totally embrace Jesus
Hell is the choice, which you have made

Written On: 2-16-15

JESUS I LOVE YOU

Jesus, I love You
That's what I thought
Yet I still had
No peace in my heart

No peace and comfort
Nor rest to my soul
I hadn't made Jesus
Lord of my life

I loved the worldly pleasures
More than I loved God
Loving the worlds things
Yes even silver and gold

Each thing I accumulated
Only lasted a short time
Then I started hungering,
Hungering for much more

One day the Holy Spirit
Tugged strong at my heart
And I surrendered everything
To the Lord Jesus Christ

I became oh so happy
Why had I waited so long
The life I'm now living
Pleases Jesus my Lord

So won't you make this day
The best for your life
Surrender all to Jesus
Give Him total control

You'll be so happy
Your life's free from sin
If you truly mean it
You'll be born-again

Heaven will await those
Who have given all to Christ
You've turned from your old ways
And now walk with the Lord

You'll then be so happy
Worshiping with all the saints
You'll love those of the world
And you'll point them to Christ

You'll not be ashamed
To spread the good news
And to share your testimony
As how you now walk with Christ

For Jesus is now
Your dearest friend
So you'll surely serve Him
To the very end

Then when the rapture
Takes place at the end of time
You'll leave this old world
In a twinkling of an eye

If you are then living
You'll move through the sky
Quicker than lighting
To meet the Lord on high

If you're in the grave
You'll come forth first
The only way I can understand it
The dead are six feet lower than everyone else

No matter what the reason
It will be a glorious day for you
Just being in the presence of Jesus
Will make living with Jesus worth while

Written On: 6-23-15

A MANSION

How often have you traveled, down a road
You see a big house on the hill
The first thing that comes out of your mouth
I love that mansion, on the hill

You dream about, the mansion you see
It plagues your mind, night and day
You have a desire for that mansion
Yes you start lusting for it

The bible plainly teaches us
We're not to want what belongs to others
If we desire what others own
It becomes sin in our life

There's nothing wrong with desiring
Something like what you just saw
But never want what others have
Yes, the bible calls it sin

Sin should never be a part of our life
For it cannot enter heaven
The bible plainly tells us
No sin will enter in

Mansions are so beautiful
Have you ever driven in a part of town?
That may be on the out skirts
Where all those wealthy people live

Those people have worked very hard
To get the big house in which they own
Yet many of those people
Are the most unhappy people in life

Why are they so unhappy?
Because their life desires more things
Yes things never satisfy
The bible makes it clear to us

Things will never satisfy
Because when you finally receive them
It only satisfies for a short time
Then you search for something more

The house which you live in
Is more exciting than the one on the hill
Because you've made the house you live in
A home, by the way you live

You may ask, "How can that be?
It's not as big as the one on the hill"
Yet you know that the Lord placed you there
So you'll make the best of what you have

Greed does not fill your life
You don't look at things, to make you happy
You know that God will keep you
On the right road that leads to heaven

You see, you've found that inner peace
Because Christ is leading your life
You desire to not get ahead of God
Desiring <u>*things,*</u> *which will grip your soul*

You see the house on the hillside
Has no peace on the inside
For Jesus is not number one
There's unsettled peace in each of their lives

When someone comes to your little mansion
Where God has directed you to live
It's filled with the peace of God
Which any one would love to have

As an unbeliever you visit them
The words that comes out of your mouth
I would give anything to have what you have
For the house is filled with peace and joy"

What he's asking is, "I will pay you
Money for what you have"
Not realizing money cannot buy
What you feel, when you walk in that house

You see the house which the believer lives in
Was filled with the presence of God
You have accepted Christ into your life
And taught it to all your family

You don't hold on tightly to your house
And the things which are therein
You would quickly give up what you have
If God should ask you to move on

Let's take a look at another mansion
Which everyone desires to have
Yet many desire to go their own way
Believing the mansion is waiting for them

That's the mansion God's preparing for us
For only the pure of heart
So if you're working for that mansion
Doing only the thing you want to do

That mansion isn't being prepared for you
For you're being a thief, trying to get in
But God looks to the enter part of your soul
To see what you have inside of you

If it doesn't measure up to God's word
Which is so important to enter heaven
The Lord will have to say to you
Your life doesn't measure up to receive

If you're living for Christ each day
Letting the Lord lead the way
Desiring all he has for you
Than walking in the path he's set for you

Then a mansion will be awaiting you
The day is not so far away
Won't you surrender all to Christ
To receive the mansion God's preparing for you

Written On: 6-9-13

YOU DON'T HAVE THE RIGHT

As a child of the Lord Jesus Christ
You don't have the right to do
Anything you want to do
As a child of the King

In Philippians2:5 we read
It's so important to a child of God
Saying, Let this mind be in you
Which was also in Christ Jesus

The verse before it, reads to us
Look not any man on his own things
But every man on the things of others
That doesn't give us room just for self

How often do people say
I'll just do what I want to do
There saying, I don't care what others think
I'll just do what I want for myself

But when we have that mind set
We're telling the Lord I'll do what I want
I don't have time to follow your directions
Which are written in your Holy Word

I have better things to do
For I know better than you
For you are old fashioned
Yes, your bible is out of date

But as the creator of this universe
Which created everything on earth
Wouldn't you think he'd provide us with
Everything we need in this life

The things we face in this life
Are trivial compared to the things
We will face when this life is over
Jesus said he'd meet our every need

So you don't have the right
To do what you want
Or you will receive the consequences
That are for your disobedient

You don't have the right to dabble with
The things of this old world
The things which gobble up your time
Which consume your time with the Lord

Yes many of the things you do in life
Are not sin within themselves
But they are sin to you my friends
You've allowed them to take the place of Christ

That's why God's word makes it plain to us
Were to work out our own salvation
Know it's not saying we can do what we want
We need to do what God has for our life

Don't depend on others to tell you
What you should do every day
But seek the Lord with your whole heart
He'll show you where you should walk

He'll lead you to read the proper things
Which will fill your mind and your soul
So you can be more like Jesus
And not like the things of this world

Yes the world has many answers
Which will lead you down the wrong path
Yes the path to destruction
And that path will lead you to Hell

What are your days, weeks, and years filled with
If the world zaps every moment you live
The world can't give you spiritual food
Which will fill your mind and your soul

Time is so important to each of us
It seems to pass by so rapidly
It's all because were filling our life
With things we should leave behind

So much of what we do are nothing but burdens
They weigh our life fully down
It's time we cast our burdens on Jesus
Rather than to allow our burdens to destroy us

Once you have given up a burden
Don't ever take that burden back
For that burden will keep getting heavier
And your life will become all messed up

You don't have the right to rob or steal
For your taking what belongs to others
And if you allow it to control your life
It will lead you straight to Hell

It's the same way with taking a life
Whether it be in the womb or not
It's still murder to the Lord
God gave the first breath, he'll give the last

You don't have the right to gossip
For gossip will hurt many people
God only gives us the right to love
Love covers a multitude of sins

There are so many things we do in life
Which hurts the heart of God
If you find yourself defying God
You must quickly repent of that sin

Sin will lead you to the pit of Hell
If not dealt with, it will keep piling up
In your life, pushing Christ away,
Soon Satan will control your life

Whether we be a Christian or not
Sin is designed to destroy you
Sin comes from the pit of Hell
It was designed to destroy your life

Won't you repent of all your sins?
Then turn from your wicked ways
Christ is standing with outstretched arms
To receive you into his fold

If you find yourself in the pit of Hell
You can blame no one but yourself
For the Lord gave you the right to chose
It's up to you to make the right choice

Written On: 5-31-15

WORDS

Have you ever, stopped to think
Of the words which you speak
Too often all the words we speak
Show how smart or dumb we are

Too often when we speak to others
We don't realize what we're saying
We fail to choose our words wisely
To make sure our words come out alright

How many words have you spoken
That hurt the hearer so much
You only wish you could take them back
Yet it's impossible for you to do

Now we search for something
We can say to patch it up
But once those words are spoken
They have pieced deep into the heart

We keep speaking other words
It keeps sending us deeper in sin
Which keeps making things worse
Rather than patch up the problem we caused

Many times we speak nasty words
For we hold bitterness in our heart
As we speak to the person we hate
We speak words which make it worse

To many surrender to the arms of Satan
By yielding to all his nasty tricks
Then we wonder why things keep getting worse
It's because we yielded to his old tricks

He says to you through your mind
Go ahead and yell back at them
Give him your peace of mind
Telling him just how you feel

But God is standing close by
Telling you to walk away
Stop and think of the words you speak
Hold your peace and don't speak them

If you listen to my still small voice
It will cover a multitude of sins
And the words in which you speak
Could cause them to surrender to Christ

They're not used to being around gentle people
Which don't lash back at them
It stops them right in there tracks
All they see is love flowing back

When you speak kind words from your heart
People take notice of who you are
They want to know what makes you tic
And they'll begin asking you questions

It's how you respond to them my friend
Which could start piercing their soul
That will change them from the inside out
So they'll surrender their life to Christ

Kind words spoken from a heart of love
Will reach multitudes of people
The Lord will use those words of love
To pierce deep in the heart of men

Real men chose their words wisely
They chose the words they speak well
They'll cover a multitude of sins
They speak forth, from a true heart of love

Won't you join the ways of Christ
Rather than the ways of the world
So the world we live in today
Will become a much better place

Today is the day to start choosing your words
To help others along the way
Slow down an choose your words wisely
And your life will be truly blessed

    Written On:10-10-13

ARE YOU A HAPPY PERSON?

All too many people on this earth
Seek for wealth and fame
They think that wealth will bring
Happiness to the life they live

Satan wants you to seek for earthly things
He tells you fame is what to look for
Yet people which seek for fame
Are the unhappiest people in this world

The jobs we seek are the type
Which bring in a lot of money
There's nothing wrong with most of them
Unless it takes you from God's will

We want that job to have benefits
And nothing is wrong with that
But what do you use the benefits for
In most cases, we use them for ourselves

You may be wondering what I mean
By using them for yourself
The reason you use them for yourself
You're so selfish in your heart

We use the sick days we have
By lying that we are sick
When all that we're using it for
Is to get a day off from work

God blesses us for only one reason
So we can lift Christ up higher
But we use our vacations for ourselves
Rather than to bless the Lord

We go off on vacation
We leave the Savior behind
We don't have time to spend in His word
For it will take from what we call fun

And of course you say when Sunday comes
God won't mind if I skip church
For He knows I need time to rest
I'll spend Sunday going out having fun

What happened to all that rest you said?
You would get while on your vacation
When you come back and go to work
It takes a week to recuperate

The Lord made sure you didn't get the rest
For you've not learnt where rest comes from
Rest comes when you're in the presence of Jesus
Yes from nowhere else my friend

Oh yes, you spend God's money
While on vacation that week
Which would keep the doors of the church open
So a bill of the church wasn't met

It just seems to not bother you
When you weren't there to teach the class
Now you've taught the new converts
That being in church just isn't important

You're teaching all those looking up to you
That faithfulness isn't important to God
When it is on God's priority list
And you're teaching new converts just the opposite

If you would have gotten excited
Of how you took time to visit another church
And how they inspired your heart real good
To prepare you when you came back home

You could have shared how you took time
Each day to read and study God's word
And how you talked to many people
About the Lord Jesus Christ

Not only did you spend time away from the church
You bought a house on the lake
Now you want to go most weekends
So you have something to brag about at work

The church is practically empty all summer
Now the church must close its doors
For you taught every other believer
Being at church and paying your tithes, isn't important

Who is it that you are fooling
Yes, it's no one but yourself
So when you get to the pearly gates
God will say I never knew you

Saying "I was looking for committed people
Who would put me first in their lives
Stranger, you can't enter
So go serve the one which you've been following"

Ones which served the Lord many years
But give up as they grow older
The Lord will have to say to you
I told you to work until you took your last breath

I was looking for those which fought the good fight
Which were always looking out for the lost
But you gave up before the battle was over
So I can't use you in the kingdom"

But there is a rest for all of those
Which fought the fight God had for them
So once they reached the pearly gates
There was a great smile on Jesus face

For the life you lived upon this earth
You always put others before yourself
Always full of the love of Jesus
You found true peace in your heart

You never failed to pay your tithes
You were always faithful to God's house
Even during your vacations
You never left Christ out of your life

You were always a joy to be around
Others loved to respect you so much
For when words came from your lips
The words lifted others up

You always strive to do your best
With what Christ had given to you
The Lord will say unto you my friend
Turn, and look behind you

You speak to God in a tender voice
Lord I don't understand all these people
God says in a kind and joyous voice
You were responsible for all of them

But Lord, I only thought I lead a few
To the cross of the Lord Jesus Christ
So where did all these people come from
I'm confused, and don't understand

Then God will speak into your heart
"Remember you always paid your tithes
So the tithes were to pay the bills
Of the church so others could worship

And remember the missionaries you supported
On those mission fields far away
Those souls they lead to Jesus
Have also become your souls

And the hungry, you reached out to feed
Allowing the love of God to flow through you
You did it from the kindness of your heart
And many came to know the Lord

Oh yes my words declare unto you
To not layup treasures upon this earth
But we're to lay treasures up in heaven
Where moth and rust can't destroy

Well that is exactly what you did
When you did everything you could
To reach those who were out in sin
Putting them before yourself

That's why you stand here today
For you did as I commanded
First to surrender your heart to Jesus
And turn from the old life you lived

You did what the bible declared of you
To following in the Lord's footsteps
You listened as the Holy Spirit tugged at your heart
Because you had started down the wrong road

You quickly asked me to forgive you
Of yielding to the ways of the world
So you were quickly placed back on track
To please me in all that you did

So because of your obedience
All these people came to know the Lord
Your eternity with me will be joyous
Welcome home my child welcome home"

This is what's called happiness
When we reach the portals of heaven
Because we have been found faithful
We can then say we're a happy person

Written On: 8-10-14

WE OWN THE BIBLE, DOES THE BIBLE OWN US

These are very powerful words
Do you know what they really mean?
Or do you look at the bible
As just another book on the shelf

Most which say they don't like it
Haven't studied the bible to know what's in it
They're so caught up in themselves
They're afraid their life will have to change

They've heard only bits and pieces
Of things people have done to others
So they make their decision by what others say
Rather than to read the Bible with an open mind

Much of the problems lie with others
There constantly squabbling among themselves
Leaving a bad taste out in the world
Leaving those of the world totally confused

We often depend on our denomination
Or the church in which we attend
To tell us how we should live our lives
We accept what they tell us as fact

When God's word makes it very plain to us
We are to study God's Holy Word
Never to take others words as truth
But prove them out by God's Word

Yes God placed the Church in order
He commissioned pastors, evangelists, and prophets
They are placed there to help guide us

Yet they also make mistakes
No we're not perfect either
We need each other to study together
And not act like a know it all
But to study together with an open mind

By studying God's word with an open mind
And others having an open mind to us
Each one may see certain things
Which the other person may have missed

Not everything in God's word
Is a fact when it stands alone
For it may depend on other scriptures
To bring the scripture to full understanding

Many a time I've been proven wrong
Or it has worked in reverse
For the Bible is like a puzzle
Which we must fit together

God doesn't give us everything on a platter
If he did we would become lazy
He expects us to study His word
So it will be planted in our heart

It's when we take God's word seriously
Share the truth wherever we go
It's when we get serious in our lives
We'll be a powerful force for the Lord

People of the world will start taking notice
That you are a true child of God
They'll then hunger for what you have
Then you can point them, to Christ

This will never happen to you
If the Bible doesn't own you
For the Bible was given by God above
To help us stay in sync with Him

It's the Bible which deals with every phase
Of our life which no other book does
It deals with children, and teenagers
Adults and every phase of our lives

It deals with everything about love
Which is a beautiful thing
If we use it as God tells us
Yes love is great in marriage

Love is more than having sex
1 Corinthians 13 tells us all about it
God wants us to love everybody
Without love, life won't fall together

It deals with us about how to vote
We must always vote the bible
If we don't vote the bible
We'll have to give an account to God

And if you fail to get out and vote
You'll be held accountable to the Lord
For your giving the election to Satan
To run the nation in which you live

The Bible is full of prophetic messages
Most have already been fulfilled
We know that Christ is coming soon
It's hard to find any passages, not fulfilled

It deals with how to find a husband or wife
And how to keep your marriage in tact
How to treat your neighbor
And how to deal with those of the world

It deals with how our lives can be blessed
First by being obedient to the Lord
By paying our tithes every week
That's how we show the Lord we love him

It doesn't matter what problems you have
If you're serious to find things out
As how to deal with them my friend
The bible covers everything in life

So the question we must ask ourselves
Do we just own a Bible?
Or do you spend much time in the word
So much, that the bible owns you

Written On: 5-21-15

THE SPIRIT OF PYTHON

Do you know what a python is?
It is a very large snake
Seeming to be very gentle
Many have python's as pets

But a python is a form of Satan
Which is so gentle you see
You would think that they loved you
When you play around with them

Many a person has picked one from a tree
They placed them around there body
Many keep them for many days
They feel the snake loves them

What they fail to realize
Is the snake is so very clever
He does not like to be trapped
So he plays along with you for weeks

One day when you took the python
Out of the cage you kept him in
You kept playing around with him
So the python wouldn't sliver away

The python seems to be your friend
You wouldn't hurt him in any way
But the python is a beast you see
And he's sly in the things he does

He has squeeze you many a time
Yet you unwrapped him from your body
So you think nothing about it
Yet one day everything changes

You're alone with the python
You get him out of his cage
But he's not the same as always
He's hungry and he needs food

You see the python is a very strong beast
This time as you wrapped him around you
Just like you had done many times before
Believing things would be the same

This time as he wrapped around you
He began squeezing you so lightly
As he squeezed you oh so slowly
Your body became numb

He knew you were not fighting back
Since your body had become numb
He squeeze you until your bones broke
Then you finally breathed your last breath

Well in case you don't understand the snake
He is a form of how Satan moves
He moves so very slowly
On a Christian which sits in the pew

When Satan tempts your life my friend
You need to quickly plead the blood
For when Satan sees the blood of Jesus
He will quickly flee from you

Yet there are too many believers
Those which have committed there life to Christ
Which are dabbling with things of this world
Then justifying it as being alright

Not realizing that Satan is very sly
He'll never deal with you harshly
For you wouldn't fall for his tactics
Then he wouldn't have a chance at you

But you can become so much stronger
As you repent of thoughts in your mind
Then you'll be a power force for Jesus
Pointing others to the foot of the Cross

Yet there are so many believers
Which yield to the tactics of Satan
Yes Satan is so very sly
He'll start wooing you to sleep

You think you can sit in the pew
Every week without any response
You would never raise your hand
Or say a hardy Amen

You're more interested in what people think of you
Than to allow the Lord move in your life
So you sit every week in the pew
Never to participate at all

You let Satan speak into your mind
Thinking about everything you'll do after church
Or what you will do next week
Or will your pot roast be burnt on the stove

You see Satan is like a python
He's so clever in all that he does
He'll fill your mind with many things
To keep you from worshiping Christ

That's the purpose we come to church
To worship the Savior of the world
But if Satan should distract you
You'll never receive anything from Christ

Then you start justifying yourself
For the things you do each day
For you have failed to receive the truth
He causes you to keep your mind off Christ

You now have the spirit of a python
Satan has you where he wants you to be
For you are now in the place
Where you will keep drifting from the Lord

If you're not going forward in Christ
Growing each day which you live
You'll lose your passion for Jesus
Then you'll become lukewarm

Lukewarm people will miss heaven
They won't be making an impact for Christ
For they are satisfied where they are
And bless God no one will move me

Once you become lukewarm
You forget to spend each day in God's word
And if you do you'll not look
For things which will improve your walk with Christ

You now sit in the comfort zone
Thinking you know all you need to know
You've read the word many times
So there's nothing more you can learn

That's when Satan has done his job well
And he has you in his grips
You'll never get back to the Savior
You've totally turned your back on Christ

Oh, you may still come to church each week
Sing the songs that others sing
You'll have no power within you
To worship the Lord from deep within

Yes you have sinned away your day of grace
Never to get back to the Lord
For God has already severed you from the vine
You've chosen Satan instead of the Lord

So if you find yourself drifting
Please get back to Christ right away
Repent of all the drifting you've done
For you don't know when you'll be cut off

And those which are serving Christ today
Won't you hunger for all Christ has for you
Seeking to always please the Lord
And not to please yourself

For when you are in the will of God
It will be the happiest place you can be
So won't you walk with Jesus every day?
You never know when your last breath will be

Written On: 3-19-14

BENJAMIN BULL FROG

Once again I was awakened
About four o'clock in the morning
And God brought to my mind
A story I'd read fifty some years ago

It was a big fat book
Which had many story's in it
Yes all of them were short ones
Just like the one I'm about to tell

He wanted to teach me a truth
To share with those in which I meet
This is how the story went
I'll tell it as close to what I can remember

The story was about a big fat frog called
Benjamin Bull Frog, and the Moon
It was about a big fat frog
Which lived in a pond out on a farm

Benjamin had many friends
Which also lived on the farm
The cows watched him in amazement
As he stretched himself out on the bank

He would sun himself during the day
As he would rest on the shore
And many of his friends would watch him
When he woke, his friends would be there

One night before he went off to sleep
He enjoyed the evening so much
For the moon was so full
It cast light far on the earth

He lay on the bank soaking in
The beauty of the evening
The moon was totally full
So he could see very far

He finally fell off to sleep
Having a very peaceful rest
But when he woke up in the morning
He couldn't believe what he saw

There stuck in the briar patch
Was the moon he had watched that night
So he went out and told all his friends
What had happened, while they were sleeping

He told them the moon had fallen
So they all came to see
The cows, the mice, and the rabbits
Squirrels, horses, and many others

Sure enough every one which came
Saw the moon lying on the ground
It brought fear, to their hearts
Knowing it wouldn't be shining any more

They watched the moon most of the day
Then a little breeze moved it back and forth
An as they watched it moving in the wind
All of a sudden the moon burst

Now they were all saddened
Each went back to where they lived
Knowing that the sky would never again
Be illuminated by the moon again

That night he lay out on the ground
So sad for what had happened that day
As he lay there something amazing happened
The moon came over the horizon

How could that ever be
For the moon had burst that very day
Was there a second moon
Which they took turns, raising in the sky

They inspected the one that had burst
They found bits and pieces on the ground
They could not understand
Why the one moon had fallen down

What they didn't know
A little boy lived on the farm
Had a balloon filled with helium
It had gotten away from him

Once the helium had seeped out of it
The balloon fell from the sky
That's just how Satan deceives us
He's got all types of tricks up his sleeve

Remember many years ago
It seemed there always were
Dates being set for Christ to return
It's a powerful trick of the devil

You may say, how can you say that
Let's take a very close look at it
Every time that Christ didn't come
It put more doubt in people's minds

People were constantly saying
That you can't trust the bible
For the Lord hadn't come back
People had deceived them for many years

But you see, they listened to people
Rather than to check the bible out
There wasn't any way, Christ could have come
Many things in God's word, hadn't been fulfilled

Remember the latest one we heard
The one most people got caught up in it
Even those which called themselves Christians
Believed this lie, Satan had placed on this earth

Everyone filled there pantries
With oh so much food for months
For they thought everything would fall apart
When the clock turned, to two thousand

Even many thought it would be the day
When the world would come to an end
Once that day came along
Each day went on just as the past

People everywhere on the earth
Got disturbed in their hearts
They said, that you can't trust a Christian
To what they say that will come to pass

But what we need to understand
The ones which believe Satan's tactics
Were people which weren't versed in the Bible
They just trusted people to tell the truth

God's word teaches us very plainly
That no one knows the day or the hour
When the Lord will come again yet we know
The season he will come, it's in God's word

How is it that we will know it?
By how prophecies have been fulfilled
Like when Israel became a nation
The bible says He will come, before that generation ends

Then put all the other prophecy's together
Which have been fulfilled in the last fifty years
By putting them all together my friend
Shows us he could come any day

Even people which sit in the pew
Are not looking for him any more
But the bible tells us so plainly he'll come
At a time, we're not looking for Him

That's why the bible tells us
There's a wide and a narrow road
That's leading to the choice you make
To the one which you make on earth

If you choice to deny the scripture
Not connected to Christ Our Redeemer
Living as the world lives, be assured
The wide road leading to hell will be yours

Those living on the wide road
Don't love the Lord with their whole heart
Spend little or no time in the Word
They just take the words of other people

That's called the blind, leading the blind
And they'll lead you straight to hell
For they don't know what the bible says
Their desire is only to please themselves

They've caved into political correctness
Trying to please everyone
God's not caring what others believe
He's concerned that you follow His Word

The one which is on the narrow road...
Yes there's very few on that road
Because our churches are full
Of lukewarm people, sitting in the pew

The lukewarm people, which God calls them,
Have no passion for the things of Christ
That's what the bible calls lukewarm
They just leave the pastor feed their soul

What they fail to realize
That the pastors are human like you and me
Yes they also make mistakes
Even when their preaching from the pulpit

Any pastor which has a compassion for Christ
Will tell them to check him out, in God's word
Don't take the pastor's word for it
We need to be driven to study God's word

Pastors, God's placed in the pulpits
To inspire us to seek the Lord
With our whole heart and soul
He's not there for us to follow him

We're only to follow his leading
As we prove it in God's Holy word
That's why there are so many splits in churches
Their eyes were on the pastor, and not the Lord

The ones which love Christ with their whole heart
Will spend much time in God's Holy word
Seeking all that Christ has for them
Desiring to measure up to the scriptures

Allowing the Lord to change their life
As they read about things they're doing wrong
For their seeking to do God's will
So they quickly change, their life to follow Christ

A true blue Christian will stop trying
To prove that they are right
By pulling scriptures out of the word of God
Which will prove their right and no one else

For you can make the Bible say
Just what you want it to say
In order to prove the point you want
Yet most times they are out of context

I see it happen all the time
People are so set in there ways
They say bless God, I've found the truth
When God is sitting back shaking His head

Every one of us has things
In our lives, which need to be changed,
It's when we think we are perfect,
Satan has your life, and you don't even know it

The Lord has taught me a principle
Which has totally changed my thinking
To stop trying to prove I'm right
But to prove Gods word is truth

You might say, what do you mean?
Let's look at it a little closer
If I've been taught something for years
And think I've got it all together

Just write all those passages down
Now take the passages which others use,
Which teaches different than you teach,
Which they each teach from God's Word

Now the next thing we need to do
Is to check to see, if they have been taken
Out of context, or used to say their right
Most you can now strike them from your list

Now, you have scriptures on both sides
God's Word says that it doesn't lie
Now we have a choice to make
Is the God of heaven a liar?

We know that God's Word doesn't lie
So maybe we're missing something
So what is the next step to make?
We need to interpret scripture with scripture

If God tells something in one passage
And something different in another
Be assured, in each, He's talking about
A specific thing, or a situation

So the next thing we need to understand
Does it say "if" in any of the passages?
If he does it means that we
Must measure up to the standards, God's word has set

If we don't measure up to his standards
Then what He's telling us it will not happen
It'll not happen to you my friend
For your not following in God's footsteps

That's why God tells us to study his word
2 Timothy2:15 reads, study to show thyself
Approved unto God, a workman that needeth not to be
Ashamed, rightly dividing the word of truth

Then we must realize all scriptures are inspired by God
And is profitable for doctrine, for reproof
For correction, and also for instruction
In righteousness....2 timothy3:16

Then in Revelation 22:19 it tells us
To not take away from, or to add to his book
If we do our name will be taken
From God's Book of Life

As you read these three passages
They seem to be a little confusing
For the one says we can use it for doctrine
The other says we can't add or subtract from it

That's why we must interpret scripture with scripture
Yes you must put your thinking cap on
Stop making it say what you want it to say
And compare the scriptures together

When it says the scripture is profitable for doctrine
For reproof, and for correction
And also for instruction in righteousness
It's not telling us to change the scripture

It's telling us to measure ourselves
Changing the things we need to change
In our life and not in the Bible
For God's Word is nothing but truth

So just as Benjamin Bull Frog
Was deceived as to what he saw
We must make sure were not deceived
In what we've believed for years

The Bible teaches that we're to hold fast
To the things we've been once taught
That's not what your parents told you
For it goes strictly against God's word

Just think if you followed your parents
Which most are living a wicked life
That's why we're in such a mess
For were following in our parents footsteps

What this is telling each of us were to
Follow what God's given us from the beginning
Following God's Word teaches everything we need
But we must read and study it each day

Then spend much time communicating with Christ
Through spending much time in prayer
Being serious in wanting all God has for you
You can be assured God will answer your prayer

He may answer you as you sleep at night
Or through someone whom God sends your way
He speaks to us through His Holy word
Or He could speak through God's creation

He could speak to you through His Holy Spirit
Yes through tongues and interpretation
Sometimes tragedy may come your way
In order for you to be brought to your knees

There are multiple ways God speaks to us
The question is, am I expecting Him to speak
If we're not expecting Him to speak
We'll probably miss His speaking to us

God loves every one of us
Yet there are those, which He spend more time with
For they make themselves available
Anytime Christ wants to speak

Too many get caught up in the cares of this world
They never have time to spend with Christ
So don't expect to make heaven
For Christ can't hear you beckoning to Him

The ones which have surrendered their life to Christ
And have turned from their past ways
Seeking all Christ has for them
Be assured heaven is awaiting them

Yes joy, and peace, you'll have in your soul
You've set the example before the world
Just as the frog could enjoy life
Finding what he thought was the moon was a balloon

God can give you peace through the storms you face
He'll send the Holy Spirit to comfort you
Won't you walk with Christ every day
Assuring you a place in heaven

Written On: 2-13-15

THE POWER OF THE END

As I go into a library
There are books everywhere you look
Which ones do I choose
I have a great choice you see

So many are they, I must chose
Which one I will take home
I begin leafing through those books
I read many captions inside them

Some of them may catch my eyes
While others I put back on the shelf
Depending on what I'm looking for
Most are put back, to not be taken home

Do I like the books of fiction?
Or ones which tell a true story
Of the lives of real people,
Most of those quickly catch your eye

You quickly read the caption,
Which is just inside the book,
It gets so interesting to you
You quickly turn to the end of the book

Most tell you, don't read the end of the book
For you spoil the story written there in
But you quickly reply to them
It helps take the stress off of my life

So often when you read the book
Of the one you have in your hands
You get so bottled up inside
You have to put the book quickly down

You can't stand all the pressure
This book's, placing on your life
It's just as if you were right there
Standing by the person in the book

But the pressure isn't so bad for you
When you read the end of the book
Knowing everything will turn out alright
For the person you're reading about.

As a believer in the Lord Jesus Christ
Who has embraced Christ in his heart?
Taking the Word of God seriously
There are so many bad things in it

As I turn to the end of the Bible
To find out what happens in the end
It tells us if were totally serving Jesus
At the end of time, we win

Now when I go back and read the Bible
Yes the Bible, God's Holy Word
I feel so much better inside
For I desire to please the Lord Jesus Christ

I want all that God has for me
I know he will help me through
The good times and the bad times
Christ is truly my dearest friend

No matter what others think of me
I'll stay true to God's Holy Word
For I know the Word is my road map
Which will lead me to heaven above

Knowing God has our best at heart
He would never lead us astray
If I should falter and fail Him
He'll pick me up if I quickly repent

Of course I must repent with a true heart
Meaning it through and through
God knows if I truly mean it
If I do, He'll quickly wipe it away

Never to remember that sin any more
It's quickly wiped from God's mind
But wait, I keep remembering my past
It keeps coming back to my mind every day

Oh yes I read in God's Holy book
Once you repent were to forget our past
So if you keep bringing it up
You've never surrendered it to Christ

Oh yes I read in God's Holy book
That Satan is the prince of the air
And he has reign, till the end of time
Then he'll be tossed into the flames of hell

What does God tell me to do?
When Satan brings up my past
Satan tells me the things of the past I've done
Just are too bad for God to forgive

Yet I remember God's word plainly tells me
If I've truly placed it under God's blood
God can't remember that sin any more
So why should I remember it again

So God's word quickly speaks to my soul
Tell Satan they're covered with the blood
Then Satan will quickly flee
He knows there's so much power in the blood

The blood can change everything
When we're serious before the Lord
So stop bringing the past sins up again
Unless it's to help someone along the way

What do I mean by helping someone?
Maybe someone is facing a similar test
Like if someone may be a thief or a robber
Show them Christ wiped your sins all away

By surrendering your life to Christ
You don't have to be tormented any more
For Christ has your best at heart
Then Satan will have to flee

Your testimony is so powerful, to others
Never falsify what Christ has done for you
A testimony shared out of a heart of love
Will show how Christ has changed your life

Won't you share your testimony
Everywhere you go in life
Never be arrogant in your sharing
But share out of a heart of love

Wait for the opportunity for you to
Share what Christ has done for you
Ask the Lord to soften someone's heart
You can share with someone today

Yes God is truly faithful
To give us opportunities each day
Don't let fear over take you
For fear is a trick of the devil

It may be hard the first time
But it gets easier each time you share
Please don't cave into fear
If you don't, it will build your faith

Always keep focused on the end of the book
Allowing Christ to lead the way
Reading, studying and praying everyday
Will help you grow in a marvelous way

Don't get discouraged if you don't make big strides
For Christ knows how fast you should grow
Everyone's pace is different
So stop comparing yourself with others

Just stay in God's will everyday
Never to lean on your own strength
You'll be preparing yourself for heaven
For the end of God's book says you win

Written On: 10- 30- 13

THE IMPORTANCE OF A COVENANT

Today we hear little or nothing
About a covenant which is so important
All is quiet, everywhere you go
For a covenant is never to be broken

All we hear about today
Is a contract which are designed to end
It only lasts for a short time
People look forward for it to end

A contract is designed by man
They only want it to last for a period of time
You, many times, can buy a contract out
And end it short of the regular time

Let's first take a look at some contracts
We go make a loan at a bank
You want to buy a car you love
And you don't have money to buy it

You go to the local bank
Ask for a loan for thirty thousand
The banker pulls out a piece of paper
Which they call a contract

They make you the loan for six years
And you sign the piece of paper
What you're telling the banker is
You'll pay it off within six years

Some take the full six years
Others only half the time
If you stop paying the payments
The car must be repossessed

Covenants are much different
Than a contract designed by man
A covenant is designed by God
God's covenant won't be broken

Let's take a look at a couple covenants
Which the Lord designed for man
These aren't ever to be broken
It's all for the good of man

Let's take a look at the first covenant
God gave to Adam and Eve
God gave a covenant to them
As he placed them in the perfect garden

There wasn't any sin in the garden
It was designed for man to live
Always to live in peace
And to live for all eternity

But Satan came snooping around
He convinced the woman to partake
Then she gave to Adam
The forbidden fruit in the garden

If Adam hadn't partaken of it
We would still be in the garden today
For God made man as the head of the home
If he had only made the right choice

God threw them out of the garden
Because of the choice Adam made
But as far as God is concerned
The perfect place is still for the end

Yes when this dispensation comes to an end
Those which have surrendered their life to Christ
Will be placed once again in the garden
Where they'll live for all eternity

A covenant has been sealed by God
God will never break what he has sealed
Yet man can break the covenant
Upon this earth which he lives

You might say, give me an example
It is so simple to understand
Yet so many will still tell you
That you can't break a covenant

When we look at someone getting married
Yes God designed marriage for man
God seals the marriage, as you say your vows
And God expects them to never be broken

Yet many get off on the wrong foot
Many marriages don't last very long
For many a marriage wasn't taken seriously
You thought you could live like before

Then others get so caught up in their kids
They don't take time for each other
So once the children leave the nest
They end up getting a divorce

When we surrender our life to Jesus
Your salvation is sealed by God
He will never let you go
He loves you owe so much

Yet if you don't stay close to the cross
Everyday keeping in fellowship with him
Each day asking Jesus to forgive you
Of sins in which you have committed

But if you allow your sins to build up
To long before you ask for forgiveness
You'll get to far from the Savior above
And you'll be too close to the world

At some point in your life
You'll stop producing fruit for the Lord
The Lord will finally cut you off
Yes it's recorded in John 15:1-6

God loves you more than you'll ever know
Won't you surrender your life to Christ
He always has your best at heart
That's why it's important to love him so

God didn't design a covenant for us to break
He has a special plan for our lives
If we stay in sync with His plan
We'll come out better on the other side

Always remember Christ is our provider
He wants us to advance in our walk with him
Sometimes the road may be rocky
But remember, he always has our best at heart

Tough times make us stronger in our walk
So stop focusing on the present
Keep focused on the final goal
We'll get through the tough times much quicker

Tough times which you face in life
Prepares you for greater things in life
It will strengthen your walk with Jesus
If you stay close to the cross

That's why God made covenants for us
The world will never understand them
For they don't understand the bible
Until they surrender their life to Christ

So let's be obedient to God's covenants
For they are designed to keep us intact
To prepare us each for heaven
To be with Jesus for eternity

So surrender your life to Jesus
Stop playing around with the things of this world
For the world doesn't mix with Jesus
Mixing them will sent you to Hell

After you surrender your life to Jesus
Spend much time with the Lord in prayer
Studying God's word everyday
Turning from the past life which you lived

Then heaven will be awaiting you
If you don't waver in your walk with Christ
If you should find yourself wavering
Quickly repent and get back to Christ

Remember Christ has your best at heart
He wants you to reach your goal
And He knows how to get you there
So always keep listening for his leading

Yes, covenants can be broken
Not on God's part, but on man's
So be careful you don't break them
For it could send you straight to hell

Written On: 5-19-15

PERFECT

How many people do you meet?
As you live your life each day,
They think that they are perfect
But you can soon see all their flaws

They think that they are perfect
Yet it's because of the standards they set
But there's not a perfect person on earth
Most don't know what perfection is

We are the perfect one in the class
What is it that made us that way?
We have measured ourselves by others
Which were in the same class

What is it that made you perfect?
You have the highest grades of all
Now, no one can reach your heart
A perfect person has their mind made up

When your mind is totally made up
You're in a very bad position
You'll never accept wise counsel
Nor can God speak to your heart

You'll miss so much in this life
Much of what you miss, are important things
Things which prepare you for eternal life
We never keep the final goal in focus

If we focus on ourselves
Our mentality is limited
For we can't think of everything
We need to live our lives

Satan has so many of us
Wooed into his little tactics
Things we never look for
For we've caved into Satan's ways

There are things which are out right sins
Then there are things which will lead you there
You may say I will take my chances
That's a place no man should want to be

We must constantly be looking for Satan's tactics
Most things he does, looks good up front
And many of the places he leads us to
Aren't wrong within themselves

Yet the problem with those things you do
Takes up all the time you have
Like sports which start out very innocent
But finally, it controls your life

You get so tied up in them
You must watch every game on TV
It started out when you were a child
Playing in those little leagues

Then it got so embedded in your soul
Even though you once loved the Lord
Oh yes you may still go to church
But it's what are you going to church for

As the preacher gives that powerful message
What the Lord had prepared for your life
But the first thing you started thinking about
Was the game you must go to after church

The way Satan works in people's lives
He'll cause a thought to come at the very time
When the preacher was speaking a powerful thing
Which would advance you in the things of Christ

But the game took priority in your life
To keep your mind off the things of Christ
Before long the game controls your life
The game now replaces the Lord

Now you only go to church
When it's convenient for you
Or you only go to church
When you must please someone else

That mentality which you now have
You know longer love Christ with all your heart
And everything you do now
Is only done to please man and self

The bible plainly tells each of us
Christ wants all of us and not just a part
When other things take priority in our life
Those other things become our god

We as a true believer in Christ,
Which has accepted Christ totally in our life,
Need to always strive for perfection
Even though we'll never arrive in our lifetime

You may say, why try
If you'll never arrive in your lifetime?
That's the beauty of serving Jesus
He always has something better for our life

We'll never know how far he'll take us
Until we strive to always seek more of him
When he has our total mind and soul
He knows he can trust us to use what he gives

Trusting us to share with others,
Which will prepare others for heaven,
That is the type person he's looking for
Committed people who truly love the Lord

We must remember that there's only one
Perfect person, to pattern our life after
Psalms19:7 tells us who to serve
It says the law of the Lord is perfect

It tells us what perfection does for us
Yes it converts the soul
It makes the testimony of the Lord sure
It also makes us wise, simple people

In other words you don't think you're above others
You're still wise to look out for the lost
To lead and teach them the ways of the Lord
That they too can be prepared for heaven

Oh yes it says in the bible that Noah
Was a perfect man and he was just
You must compare scripture with scripture
To understand what it's talking about

When you study the bible completely
He's talking about yielding totally to him
He desired all God had for his life
The things of this world took second place

When God's word teaches us in 2 Coth.13:11
Paul closes out this book by giving this message
Saying finally brethren farewell
The brethren he's talking about are believers

He says be perfect and be of good comfort
Be of one mind to live in peace
Then the God of love and peace will be with you
Yes in each of us to do God's will

When He's talking about God's love
God's word is important to a saint of God
For the world is filled with false love
Satan will lead you down the wrong road

What this message is saying, be ye perfect
It doesn't mean we will arrive
But we're to strive to be perfect like Jesus
And we'll then be on the right path

So won't you daily strive for perfection?
Yes, follow Christ every day that you live
Then when this life on earth is over
The Lord will usher us into heaven

Written On: 8-31-14

DO YOU HAVE AN OPEN LINE?

How many times have you
Went to the telephone
And picked it up to make a call?
There wasn't a dial tone, to be heard

You became so disturbed
For the call was so important
Maybe a life, was at stake
But the line, has been broken

You may have had a fire
And you couldn't call 911
So because the line was broken
Your house was burned down

You may have had, to make a call
To that place where you, were looking for a job
But the dial tone, wasn't there
So you missed the job, you needed

You may have gone to your computer
To look up something important
But you couldn't get on line
For it kept saying, you weren't connected

How many times, has the line been broken
Between, a husband and a wife
Because you wanted, your own way
Rather than sit down, and talk things out

You fumed for days and weeks
Because you decided, it was only your way
You never thought things through
Which could solve, the whole problem

A teenager blocks communication
Between their mom and dad
They think they know, what's best
In the situation, which they're in

That's why God, gave us parents
Because of wisdom, they have received
They see things, which the child can't see
Let's stop breaking, communication with them

There's a more important line,
Which is always opened,
But we can break that connection
Because we fail to communicate

It's so important that we keep connected
For many problems would never come
But we fail to speak to him
That connection is the Lord Jesus Christ

We wake up in the morning
Failing to speak to Him
Because we can only think
Of the busy day ahead

We fail to realize
If we talked to the Father above
He'd guide us through the busy day
And things would run more smoothly

You see, the Lord has all the answers
To the problems we face in life
And when that problem comes
He can guide us straight through it

The problem is, when we don't
Give Him the first fruit of our life
And only give Christ the left overs
Be assured, problems will multiply

God said, He would always be there
To take our hands, and walk with us
But when we fail, to speak to Christ
Before we start, the day

We have broken the communication line
Not the Lord, for He's still waiting
But He can't help you, through your problems
Because you decided, to do it your own way

Won't you get your life in order,
Surrendering your whole life to Christ
Allowing the Holy Spirit to guide you
Not pushing the Holy Spirit away?

Giving Christ, number one position
In your life, as you start each day
Living for Christ, throughout the day
Then closing the day, by talking to Him

Then when you lay your head to rest
Your mind, can be relaxed
For you have complete, peace of mind
For you've not, closed Jesus out

The line to heaven, is always open
But too often, we fail to pick it up
My friend, won't you keep the line open
You'll be so happy, you didn't hang up

Written On: 12-2-11

MANY CALL THEMSELVES CHRISTIAN

No matter where you go in life
People say that they're a Christian
Whether they are in the work place
Or even in the church

They love to be called a Christian
For it makes them feel so good
Yet so many, or most of them,
Haven't a clue what being a Christian is

Just because they were born in a Christian family
And have gone to church all their life
Doing everything a Christian does
They each think that they're all right

You talk as other Christians do
You even teach a Sunday School Class
You could even be a preacher
So you think everything is alright

You teach the boys or girls class
Everyone even looks up to you
For you've done it for so very long
Everyone thinks that you are great

You have been a part of the church
Because of all the good things you do
You reach out to meet the needs of others
Yet there is emptiness in your heart

The church you've picked is just like you
They love meeting the needs of others
So you think that makes you a Christian
Because you have joined the church

Many join the church and take communion
Go through all the rituals which they do
Yet there is emptiness inside
You just seem to not be able to figure it out

You would never go to another church
Where the power of God is moving
For you had been taught all your life
To never visit any other congregation

So you only hear what the denomination teaches
Did you ever stop to think, they could be wrong
So you never check out their teachings with the bible
You just take their word, that they are right

It's time to check everyone out
As to what they each are teaching
Whether an individual or denomination
They could be part of Satan's plan

You never pick up your bible
To measure their teachings with God's word
So you're like the blind, leading the blind
That's how Satan wants us to live

Many call themselves Christian
Because they were born in the USA
Yes it was founded on Christianity
They think that will lead you to heaven

This nation has wavered so far from God
You never check the government out with the Bible
So you take the laws of our government
As things in which we have to follow

But God's word teaches us
We're only to follow them as they measure up
With God's Holy Word
If they don't, we're to follow God's leading

So were selling ourselves to Satan
You can't talk about the government in the church
Unless you're on Satan's side
Then you can talk about it all you want

That alone is a red flag
For they're only picking out one group of people
And the only one that can't speak
Is the one that is showing the true love of Christ

The reason the world is getting so much grip on us
The church has let their guard down
We've become nothing more than a social gathering
And Christ isn't allowed in the church

No, most people that call themselves Christian
Are very far from the Lord
They've never experienced the power of Christ
For they'd be controversial to the world

Yes, following Jesus is a rough road to follow
Most people won't make it to heaven for they
Don't want to be confronted about their life
So they just blend in with the crowd

Jesus said if you're ashamed of me
I'll also be ashamed of you
Then you'll not make it to heaven
For you've compromised the Christian life

That's why the road to heaven
Is a very, very narrow road
For most people which think they're on it
Are on the wide road to hell

A Christian is a Christ follower
Which doesn't walk in his own strength
But leans upon the word of God
And allows the Lord to lead the way

Yes, you might be made fun of
And persecution may come to you
But remember life here upon this earth
Is short compared to eternity

The question each must ask himself
Where do I want to spend eternity?
The choice is up to each of us
It's our choice and not someone else

Serving Jesus is the only way
We'll find it in God's Holy Word
How we can get to heaven
We need to read it to find out

It says everyone must make their own choice
By repenting of all their past sins
Then we're to turn from our old ways
An embrace Jesus with all our heart

Then there are requirements after redemption
We need to read and pray every day
Asking Him to speak to you through the bible
What you need to change in my life

If you don't do it every day
You'll soon fall by the wayside my friend
Then eventually you'll fall from the grace of God
Then God will have to cut you off

Unproductive people, God can't use
What's the decision you will make?
The choice is either heaven or hell
God's beckoning for your call

Written On: 10-9-13

WHEN ARE YOU GOING TO GET SERIOUS

This nation is full of people
Which live their lives in a non-serious way
They think their alright living their lives
Any way in which they desire

Each make up their own standards
In which they say they'll live by
The question is, are these standards
According to the word of God?

This is what is driving my mind
Are we as a church, serious in our walk with Christ?
Are we really serious in going to heaven?
When we look at things the church is doing

The bible makes it very clear
There's a wide and narrow road
The wide road leading to hell
The narrow road leading to heaven

When you look at how most churches treat God
It's a soft coated message which most portray
We tend to put most people in heaven
That's why the churches are so weak

They're not taking the Bible seriously
It seems that everything is alright in the church
Let's take a look at how people look at it
Hopefully you'll understand where I'm coming from

If you take what all the people say
Yes preachers from pulpits across the land
Telling you how millions every year
Are getting saved and ready for heaven

If all of these people are getting saved
Wouldn't you think that this nation would be
Much safer as we live each day and week
But it's getting worse as each day passes by

The people which say they're a Christian
Have little concern about the things of God
It's hard to get them to stand up for righteousness
They tend to sit back and relax

Saying everything will turn out alright
Let's go to church to feel good
So they walk into the church each week
Leaving the church, the same way they came

What do I see with this generation?
They don't take their walk with Christ seriously
Few spend much time in the bible
And less and less time in prayer

You say, how can I say that?
You don't know the lives of each of them
Yet the bible makes it very plain to us
That we'll know them by the life they live

Just look around at most people
Which say that they're a Christian
When they come to church each week
There ashamed to carry their bible

We've made it so easy for everyone
We put the scriptures on the wall
Or we only use our cell phone
To say that we own a bible

Are we ashamed of the Bible?
Yes the precious word of God
The message we are giving the world
The Bible isn't precious to us

Then people which go to the alter
There's no remorse for their actions
They go to the alter often
Then leave the alter the same way they came

They're not serious in their relationship
With the Savior and Lord of the world
We know because our churches have little power
We're not making an impact in the world

Just call a prayer meeting
Hardly anyone will come to it
Yet have a supper at the church
People who rarely come, will surely be there

In our Sunday night services
You find very few people there
You're not setting the day aside
You're using the day to catch up on your work

You use the excuse that it's the only time
I have to work around my home
For it is the only day I have for myself
So I have to use it to get my work done

Why don't you use your evening
Or Saturday to get your work done
Using Sunday for your day of rest
And be fed from God's Holy Word

It's all about where your priorities are
Are they to serve Christ or the World?
I'm afraid the priorities of most people
Are for self, instead of the Lord

That's why there are so many lukewarm people
It's about people which can't make up their minds
As who is number one in their life
It's mainly about the world, instead of the Lord

Who or whatever has your attention
Yes, what takes priority in your life
Has become the god in which you serve
For most are serving the devil

You may say how can you say that?
God says He'll only be number one
So why don't things of Christ
Take priority over the world

Most people which call themselves Christian
And won't talk to people out in the world
They say it should be kept in the church
Then everything will work out alright

If this is the attitude which you have
Not making Christ number one in your life
Be assured you won't make it to heaven
You will end up in the pit of Hell

It's time to get back to the bible
Our life here on earth is about to end
When we see all the prophecy's which have been fulfilled
It's hard to find any not fulfilled in God's Word

Serving Jesus is so very important
It's the only way we can get to heaven
Without being serious in serving the Lord
You'll not have a chance to make it there

Yes, every one of us makes mistakes
Yet Christ is looking for a repentant heart
Which most people, which call themselves Christian,
Spend their days trying to justify themselves

God's not interested in your thinking
He's interested in you following His word
And if you should falter along the way
You need to quickly repent of your past

Then serve the Lord with your whole heart
Getting back to the principles in God's Word
Not allowing the world dictate to you
As how you will live your life

If the world should come against you
Are you willing to serve the Lord?
Even if your life should be taken
Are you willing to fight, till you take your last breath?

That's what the Lord expects of any Christian
That we spend time with the Lord every day
Praying and reading God's Holy Word
Asking the Holy Spirit to lead the way

Spending valuable time in the house of God
Expecting to receive, to help you grow in the Lord
Searching for things you need to change in your life
And quickly change to measure up to God's Word

I see very little effort in most churches
To preach upon morals, we are to follow
We have left our guard down
And replaced them with all types of programs

Most programs are about having fun
Rather than to strengthen people in the Lord
It's time all our programs be strengthened
With Christ being the center of them all

The reason most programs will not change
The leaders are not even Christians
But their living a form of Godliness
Deceiving the children in which their teaching

The world is all about having fun in life
And keeping you away from the house of God
The enemy knows if he weakens the church
He'll have most of the people in the world

The thing we need to decide is
Am I serious in my walk with the Lord?
Will you turn from the ways, of the world
Putting Christ first place in all that you do

It's then your life will be filled with knowledge
Christ will see you through to the portals of heaven
And once we get filled with the Spirit
It will roll out into the world

That's when the world will begin to change
Yes revival will start taking place
Then Christian's will begin making an impact everywhere
They set their feet and Christ will be lifted up

Are you ready to surrender all to Jesus?
To walk with Christ, every day that you live
So you'll be ready to enter the portals of heaven
When the rapture takes place or death should come

Written On: 10-22-15

MARRIAGE

We seek to improve our life
So we can receive prestige and fame
Feeling that our pocketbooks
Will broil over and will get rich

We seek fame in so many ways
So we'll be accepted in this life
We feel that if were accepted
We will have many friends

We intentionally leave the Lord out
Feeling we can make it on our own
Failing to realizing, if it wasn't for God,
We wouldn't accomplish anything in life

In order to climb the ladder in life
We can't sit back and dream about it
But we must work very hard
In order to climb each step we take

Sometimes it may require more college
And many seminars along the way
In order to understand more about
The position we seek in life

We strive to do our best
To impress higher ups along the way
So we don't spend our life goofing off
Knowing it will hinder us from climbing the ladder

Once you start doing extras
Without expecting extra pay for it
The boss takes notice you're serious
To advance yourself in life

Life is so important to us
Yet too many are married to their job
Letting the most important things
Lay aside, from the life you live

We separate ourselves from our spouse
Not giving them the attention they need
For we think it's more important
To climb the ladder to advance your life

There are ways to advance in this life
Without destroying our own flesh and blood
That's to seek the Lord with your whole heart
Then he may take you in another direction

You see the directions which you face in life
May not be where God wants you to go
Because it will lead you from the cross
Sending you straight to hell

All because you become puffed up
Thinking you have everything in your control
So you don't trust the Lord to lead you
As you live your life on earth

God may be saying to you
Turn from the direction you're headed in
For the call of God is upon your life
To be a servant of the King

You heed the call of God on your life
And follow the direction he's leading you
At the very time God is calling you
He's also probing the heart of your spouse

You both sit down and talk it out,
Which is the sensible thing to do,
And after each tell their story
How the Holy Spirit probed their heart

They then knew it was God, probing them
To change direction for their lives
Knowing that when it is the will of God
Everything will fall right in place

The first person which looked at their house
Bought it for what they asked for it
Doors opened for them to go
To Africa yes the mission field

God gave them such a peace of heart
The Lord wouldn't speak to one and not the other
So they began walking in the same direction
And everything just flowed together

But the organization said, they were too old
To go to the mission field
But that didn't stop them
For they knew they were in God's will

The doors for them finally opened
For when God says yes, he'll provide the way
And the minds of those on the mission board
Changed their minds, and gave them the green light

The people on the mission field
Opened up to them with open arms
And multitudes came to Jesus
Because of their obedience to the Lord

Oh yes there were stumbling blocks
Along the path which they trod
Yet a peace came to each of them
They were assured they were in God's will

They had such a peace among those people
They never even came back home
For the money God kept sending in
To help them stay on the mission field

Life finally came to an end
And they were buried on the mission field
Then the leaders which were taught by them
Carried the message of Christ to that nation

Multiplication kept moving on
Because of two people which heeded God's call
And now the message of Christ is so powerful
Because of two people obedient to God's call

Are you following the will of God
Listening for Christ to speak to your heart
For if we're obedient to Christ
We can know we're in God's will

You may never become a preacher or teacher
Or a missionary in a faraway land
Yet God also needs committed people
Which will serve Christ where they are

All God asks of each of us
Is to be obedient to his call
And be assured, God will go before you
No matter the direction, which he'll send you

Marriage is not just between husband and wife
But there is something even more important
That's being married to Christ
Every day in which you live

Written On: 8-22-13

THE LORD WANTS TO DO GREAT THINGS

The Lord wants to do great things
In the life in which you live
Yet too often we limit Him
Because our life is filled with sin

How big is the God you serve?
People in churches limit him every day
That's why we don't make an impact
In the world in which we live

We are filled with too much of our thinking
So our thinking stays too small
Our minds are filled with doubt and fear
Christ can't do what he wants through us

Someone asks us to pray
For a great need they have in their life
And the first thing that grips our mind
Is that I can't pray for the needs they have

The words I have in my vocabulary
Aren't the ones I need to pray
So doubt is what controls your life
That's nothing more than a lie from Satan

You see Satan doesn't want you
To do greater things in Jesus name
For it makes him feel much smaller
For the Lord's greater in the life you now live

Many think it takes a powerful prayer
One with all those descriptive words
Ones which make people think
Their education is very great

Yet words don't have any impact
In the prayer in which you pray
If the words aren't prayed from your heart
Leaving the Savior work through you

Casting aside all of your doubts and fears
And surrendering your total life to Christ
Not wanting to take credit for your self
But giving all glory and honor to Christ

When our mind is totally focused on Jesus
We no longer want self to be praised
Letting the faith of the Lord
Take total control of our life

That's when the Lord can use us
In the world in which we live
For people know longer see us
But the Savior in which we embrace

That's when the Lord can use us
In ways we've never been used before
For you'll not limit God to the way you think
You now put on the mind of Christ

You have accepted Christ into your heart
Yet he wants to take you to higher heights
He wants to fill you with his Holy Spirit
Yes the evidence you're filled, is speaking in tongues

People say it's not for us today
That's nothing more than, Satan speaking through you
For he knows you'll be taken to higher heights
To do a greater work for Christ

God's word says this will happen in the last days
We know we're living in the last days
For prophets and men of God
Can't find many passages that haven't been fulfilled

Go ahead and listen to the voice of Satan
But Satan is a liar from the pit of hell
Yet God has your best interest at heart
He wants to take you to greater heights in Him

God will take you to higher heights
When we put on the mind of Christ
And put Satan under your feet
Covering your life with the blood of Christ

You don't have to be a powerful preacher
Or a great teacher of God's Holy Word
But a vessel surrendered to Jesus
So He can work through your life

You may be a very shy person
You can't speak to others my friend
So you say I can't speak out for Jesus
The word says, I can do all things through Christ

The only thing that's holding you back
Is letting fear grip your soul
When God is saying to you my friend
It's time you step out for me

Won't you step out of your comfort zone
Doing something you've never done
When you start doing little things
You'll be surprised, what you can do through Him

He'll then take you to higher heights
You'll be surprised when your shyness disappears
You say it can't happen to me
That's nothing more than a lie from hell

God's word says trust me each day
Rather than the voice of the world
For I will go before you
Leading you to heights you've never been before

God says He'll take you to higher heights
Yes to places you've never been
He'll not take you to unpleasant places
But places to lead you closer to heaven

And then the places you will go
Will be places that lead others to Christ
That's the desire God has for your life
And eventually lead you to heaven

So don't limit yourself to what you can do
But surrender your whole life to him
Then He will use you in so many ways
That's why Satan wants to drive you from Christ

Christ will take you to higher heights
Don't worry where he'll take you
Allow Christ lead you each day you live
Then Christ will be well pleased with you

Written On: 3-16-14

THE SWORD

When we take a look at a sword
Swords are used for different things
It can be used to encourage you
Or it can be used to destroy your life

The first thing most think about
When the word sword is brought up
Is a sword in which soldiers used
In battle to destroy other's lives

We think of those in the Old Testament
Which went to battle, yes to war,
The sword was used against the enemy
To kill the ones fighting them

Yes, today our soldiers don't carry them
They use other things in their place
They will carry a grenade along with them
Which will destroy many more lives

But back in those early days
The sword was the most powerful
Of weapons which was available
When the army went to war

Then you may watch those men
Which entertain people with their swords
Each man uses a sword
Trying to keep the other from them

As each sword tries to get you
You take your sword to deflect the other
You stop the sword from getting to you
So your life will be spared

Yes you're taught how to not
Hurt the other playing the game
You spend many hours practicing
Before you go out to entertain the crowd

A warrior's sword is used to hurt another
Yes, to place the sword into another's chest
You use it to kill that one
Which is fighting against you

We hear of men which use knives
Which is a form of a sword
They stab people which they hate
Doing it to prove they're the greatest

They feel others will fear them
If they succeed in getting to them
They only want their own way
So they put fear in others hearts

This is how Satan destroys people
Yes he's a thief and a robber
So he will do everything to deceive you
To follow in his footsteps

He does this to destroy people's lives
He doesn't want you to make it to heaven
So he'll do whatever it takes
To deceive you straight into hell

Let's take a look at a more powerful sword
Which is available to everyone
The Word is so powerful
It can bring Satan to his knees

It can stop Satan in his tracks
When he comes snooping around
God wants us to use His sword
To stop Satan from advancing on your life

This sword is the Word of God
Which can pierce deep in the heart of man
It pierces deep down in the heart
Of the person which is effected

God gave us his Holy Word
To be planted down deep in our heart
That means we're to study it
Every day in which we live

Asking the Lord to feed your soul
And reveal his word to you
Planting the Word down deep in your soul
So we can draw from, when we need it

If you don't have it in your soul
There's nothing for God to pull from
Then He can't give you the proper words
To pierce the heart of another's life

Like a person comes to talk to you
About taking something from work
God may give you the perfect scripture
In order to pierce the heart of them

Most people which talk to you
It's about bragging what they have done
They think they've done nothing wrong
For the boss didn't pay them enough

God may give you words to speak
Telling what they've done wrong
It wasn't really about that person
But what they've done is against God

A scripture might pop in your mind
The Bible tells us not to steal
Followed by such a scripture
That you shouldn't covet what others have

And if you do these type of things
God's word says we will have to pay for them
Like you may end up getting sick
Or have to replace the car you drive

You see God has everything in control
No matter what you may think
There are consequences for everything
Yes, everything we do on earth

Yet if we choose to do the things of God
Blessings will come to our lives
Yes blessings will come to our lives each day
And joy will flood our soul

There's nothing more exciting
Then to be in the perfect will of God
That's when were invited into the inner court
And the communion is fabulous for us

The inner court is better than the other one
That one is where unbelievers go
You never find peace and rest
For Satan has nothing to satisfy

When you pick up the Sword of the Spirit
God's word says take my word seriously
For it has everything you need
To walk a pure life on this earth

No matter what you do in life
Make sure you are in God's Will
That's where you'll find peace and rest
Being in the perfect presence of God

Remember the Sword of the Spirit is powerful
The Sword is God's Holy Word
It's not to be left on the shelf
Or you'll miss God's will for your life

It's when you approach the Word of God
With a desire to be taught by the word
Be assured you'll receive just what you need
For every moment you face in life

The word of God is so powerful
It will change a sinner into a priest
For a murderer he can change their heart
To be a powerful testimony to the world

Yes God is the one which changes man
Into someone which will bless others
For it is God which sees the potential in you
And He'll change your life when you trust him

So don't ever fail to hold onto
The greatest book of all times
It has stood the test of time
When man tried to do away with it

So walk with the Lord everyday
Expecting him to guide your life
You'll then be the happiest person
That ever lived upon this earth

Written On: 6-8-15

THERE'S POWER IN THE BLOOD

The powerful force of the blood
Yes, the blood in each of our veins
Has more power than we can comprehend
It's the blood that keeps us alive

Just allow the blood drain from your veins
Through an accident of some kind
And as the blood gushes from your veins
You get weaker as each moment passes by

But if someone comes along my friend
And stops the bleeding of that wound
To stop the blood from flowing
It give you time to get to the hospital

Then as they give you more blood
You begin to perk up again
For the blood gives us life
It's like you've been born-again

But there's another blood more powerful
The blood of Jesus sets men free
That's why Jesus went to Calvary
So whosoever will, can be set free

When Jesus went to that old rugged cross
It wasn't a tragedy my friend
For Jesus went to that cross willingly
He could have stopped it at any time

By calling ten thousand angles
To rescue Him from that cross
Man could never have stopped Him
But He chose to follow through with it

By completing that great sacrifice
Willing that no one would perish
He went down to the pit of hell
Grabbing the keys to the bottomless pit

Satan will be bound for eternity
When this life comes to an end
Man will no longer be tormented
For a child of God has been set free

Jesus blood that was shed at Calvary
Was so powerful that all could be free
But we must choose to go to the Cross
So Jesus can wipe away all our sins

It is Jesus blood which He shed at Calvary
That made it available for each of us
But we must accept Christ into our heart
So that we can be born-again

It's his blood which sets us free
Yes He'll wipe away all our past sins
Never to remember them again
What a great sacrifice, He made for you and me

Won't you come to that Old Rugged Cross
To be set free from all your sins
So you can have a joyous here after
With Jesus, for all eternity

Written On: 10-18-15

A ROCK

As the word rock is spoken
Our mind goes in many directions
A rock is used for many things
Let's take a closer look

How often have you heard the statement?
You have a large rock on your finger?
They're referring to that ring
Which you wear with a diamond in it

There are those which collect stones
They come in so many sizes
Along with many colors
Yes there beautiful to the eye

There are quarries around the world
Let's mention just a couple
They dig lime stone from the ground
Then crush it into many sizes

Some are used to build our roads
Many ditches are lined with them
To keep the ditches from washing away
As big storms come along

We all ride on blacktop surfaces
There filled with mostly lime stone
With pitch to hold them together
There enjoyable to ride on

Then you have the sand mines
They crush those large sand stones
Which are used in many things
Which everyone really enjoys

They wrap around all our towns
And most floors you walk on
Then buildings around this nation
All built from sand from the ground up

There are so many other stones
Yes types which I have not mentioned
All types of stones are important
Taken from within the ground around the world

There is an important rock
Which is more important than them all
You may say what type of rock is it
Let's zoom in a little closer

That rock is Christ Jesus
Which is the Savior of our soul
He's never lied to any one
And assuredly knows what's best for us

He didn't go to the cross in vain
He died, was buried and arose again
He didn't have to go there
Yet He chose to go for you and me

He was the only perfect sacrifice
That can save us from our sins
It's important to embrace this sacrifice
Which can save everyone from hell

Yet it doesn't come automatically
We must be serious from our heart
Asking Christ to save us from our sins
Then if were serious, He'll come in

He's stronger than any stone
Dug from the ground on earth
He's so powerful everywhere
To free every man, woman, and child from sin

Won't you get connected to the solid rock,
Christ Jesus, who can rescue you from Satan's grip
Your life will take on a new meaning
You'll then be preparing your life for heaven

Everyone which accepts Christ into their heart
Then turns from the past life they've lived
Be assured that Christ will rescue you
From the grip Satan has on you

Then if you follow his leading
Until your life on earth is through
You'll be assured of a great here after
In the presence of our Savior and King

Written On: 4-19-15

THE LAST LAUGH

People every day in life
Try to get the last laugh
They are in the midst of people
Talking about a certain subject

They tend to want to stand out
So they keep butting in
Trying to get their thought heard
Weather it's relevant or not

Because you're not willing to listen
You just want to get your thought through
You'll then get very upset
If you can't get your own point across

Have you ever talked to a person
That thinks their thoughts are the best
Press in to get there thought across
They put their foot in their mouth

They don't care what others think
So they speak out of turn
Then the thing which they spoke to you
Gave you the last laugh

There our people in the world
That think there the only one right
So they will do everything they can
In order to get there point across

They don't care whether they're right or wrong
If they would only take time to listen
They could see where their wrong
They have taken only one passage as truth

Much of the word depends on other passages
Like the Ten Commandments, thou shalt not steal
That's talking about you as a person
You are not to kill because of bitterness in your heart

When it comes to defending your family
Or when you're called to defend your nation
It's all right to kill them
For God has sent many into battle

When David faced Goliath
Who was defying the Israelites?
God knew there was a man
He could send to kill that man

You see God had been preparing David
Along with all the Israelite Army
But all that the people could comprehend
Is David, with one sling and three stones

They didn't know the God we served
God said he would go before us
If we will surrendered to Jesus
The battles He will fight for us

David didn't go to battle on his own
But the God of the universe was on his side
David picked up three smooth stones
Which God had placed there before him

With no armor and all that other garb
That all soldiers would wear
He proceeded to complete the task
That God has sent him to glorify Him

So David placed the stone in his sling
Swung the sling round and round
God had prepared him for this day
When he had killed a lion and a bear

The stone hit Goliath in the forehead
The only exposed part of his body
Then David quickly cut off his head
He gave all glory to the Lord

Goliath thought he would get the last laugh
If he slew David, such a little child
He had made fun of Israelites
For sending a little child to fight him

The laugh ended, at what took place
Before their very eyes
You see it was a miracle from the Lord
Using a puny boy David, to accomplish it

At the very end of time
It will be God that we'll get the last laugh
If you live your life defying God
Putting self, first in your life

The last laugh God will have
If you defied the King of Kings
For your defying the gift of salvation
Which was freely given to whosoever would come

Christ didn't go to the Cross
For only a small group of people
But the offer is made for everyone
Who will surrender all to Christ?

The last laugh God will have my friend
For thinking you know more than God
The one who created the whole universe
And always wanted the best for us

Yet you defied all he had for you
It's not God that sent you to hell
You sent yourself there my friend
You just wouldn't surrender all to Christ

You grabbed on to the world's ways
Satan is the one controlling you
You thought you knew what was best
Rather than yield your total life to Christ

You now have a choice to make
Will I begin a new life in Christ?
Living for Christ to the fullest
Following God's Holy Word

Or will you choose the broad road,
Which most people on earth are on,
Which leads to everlasting punishment
Never to enjoy life again

Don't put it off another moment
Give your life to Christ today
You'll never regret you made that choice
Here on earth and in the hereafter

Written On: 5-25-14

THE GOOD SHEPHERD

A Shepard is so important to us
Yes more than you'll ever know
Yet many are following shepherds
Which are deceiving them along the way

Deceiving shepherds are from Satan
Satan will trick you any way he can
That is what Satan's job is
To try and make us think he is God

A deceiver never lifts up the Lord
He's there to lift up himself
He thinks he's much better than God
The God of the whole universe

There are false shepherds in pulpits
All across this land and the earth
Satan sends his imps around this land
To try an deceive true servants of God

That's why it's important to study God's word
His word he sent for you and me
So we can learn to pick out
False servants on this earth

If we have the word of God
Hidden down deep in our soul
Having a true relationship with the Lord
By having fellowship with him in prayer

We'll learn quickly to spot a false Shepherd
For the Holy Spirit will quickly nudge you
That you're headed down the wrong road
Won't you quickly turn from the voice of Satan

The true Shepherd will take you to places
Where you would never think you would go
For the true Shepherd's looking out for you
So you can impact the lives of others

A true Shepherd will never teach you
To live your life for yourself
But when you learn to reach out to others
Your life will never go void

God will go with you through hard trials
Helping others, will build your life up
It will give you power in your life
Beyond where you will ever know

Don't ask how the Good Shepherd does it
It's not important to know how it's done
But to know that the Lord is faithful
Knowing he will not let you down

As long as you're in the will of God
Be assured God is on your side
He wants you to succeed in your life
Remember he created you

When you walk with the Good Shepherd
He'll lead you where you need to go
No, He'll never lead you astray
He always has your best at heart

Then you can always be assured
He'll always feed you the best in life
He'll never give you second hand things
For he wants you to grow real strong

But always stay close to the Good Shepherd
By reading and studying God's word
And communication with him everyday
By spending valuable time in pray

Then you can always be assured
That you're on the narrow road
And heaven will be awaiting you
When you finally take your last breath

Or should the rapture take place today
You don't have to live always wondering
Whether you'll make it to heaven or not
You can be assured if you walk with the Lord

Written On: 6-30-14

AN APPETITE

How often do each of us
Have an appetite for food we desire
Your appetites keeps nagging at you
You just can't wait till you feed it

People have appetites for so many things
You may have a craving for some type of sweet
Sometimes we need to control ourselves
When a craving comes to our life

We know that sweets aren't good for us
They cause us to put on all that weight
So it's important to control that craving
That keeps you wanting to reach out for more

How often has moms craved for something
While they were great with child
They craved for some type of food
That may or may not be good for them

For some they crave for some type of sweets
So we pamper them with all types of them
It could be too much sugar for that mom
That could affect both mom and the child

Or it could be causing you to put on weight
Which you won't be able to shed off
We must learn to control ourselves
When we crave for something in our life

How often do both men and women
Crave for that next cigarette
Which is destroying their lungs
And you also have bad breath

Because of that craving for cigarettes
As a young child you feel so cool
You want to blend in with the crowd
You smoke them, until you become hooked

They put something into that cigarette
So you won't want to give them up
Then as you get older in life
You end up with Asthma in your life

Some take on the craving for alcohol
You must have another drink
Now you become an alcoholic
With cirrhosis of the liver

It keeps eating at your liver
You really want to give it up
But the friends in which you've picked
Keep begging you to have another drink

You keep drinking all through life
You lose your family, and all your friends
All because you gave into the first drink
Just to fit into the crowd

There's a craving we all should reach for
That's a craving to serve the Lord
A craving to want more of Jesus
And accept him down deep in your soul

The more that we crave for Jesus
The deeper he's planted in our heart
So there isn't any room for Satan
For Jesus is number one in your life

The ways of the Lord have filled your life
Yes, replaced your old life of sin
With the word, Jesus has sent to you
And now you are free from the world

The world has nothing to long for
It leads you down the wrong path
The path that leads you to destruction
Yes your final destination is hell

Our time we live upon this earth
Is wasted if you serve the world
But a life lived totally for Jesus
Prepares you for a new life in heaven

There are few that will make it to heaven
Even though most think they'll make it there
If you can't surrender to Christ down here
Heaven for you would be a miserable place

Yes you would be miserable in heaven
If you don't love the Lord here below
You'll beg the Lord to leave you in
He'll say depart from me, you didn't love me before

But the child of God which has a big appetite
For all that the Lord has designed for him
When this life on earth is complete
The Lord will say, welcome home my child

Written On: 6-15-14

DISEASES

Diseases we find everywhere
Too many people live in fear
Believing one day they will catch one
Because diseases are everywhere

God tells us in his Holy Word
One reason we get those diseases
Proverbs 23:7 tells us plainly
As a man thinketh in his heart, so he is

So the bible is telling each of us
Don't dwell upon bad things
For if you keep dwelling on them
You may eventually catch them

Most diseases we bring upon ourselves
We do things which feed them
By eating so many unhealthy foods
Then we blame our disease on God

To many of the foods we eat
Has no nutrition in them
Then our body becomes so week
And we eventually become sick

Most of the foods in which we eat
Are nothing more than fillers
With a little flavor on them
To make us think it's good for us

Diseases are caused by so many things
It could be the air we breathe
For diseases float through the air
Driven by the wind, which we feel

Diseases come at the most unusual time
One moment you may be feeling fine
And just a few moments latter
You can end up very sick

Some people rarely get sick
For they've learned to take care of their body
They eat very nutritious food
Which builds up their immune system

Most people live from day to day
Not studying the foods which they eat
The Bible teaches that things come on us
Because of lack of knowledge

We fail to read about things on health
To find out the things we can do
We tend to believe that our doctor
Will give us the right things to heal

Doctors don't know everything
People believe in doctors, as they do there pastor
Putting their trust in the person
Rather than in the Lord Jesus Christ

There is a greater disease which many have
That's the disease of Satan, the prince of the world
People are compromising their life
Giving into the snares of the devil

Compromising their lives they live each day
Which causes them to become lukewarm
In their lives they live each day
Not following the path of Jesus Christ

The disease in which they now have
It' a very plain disease of self
Compromising their walk with the Savior
Not totally committed to Christ

You once had a great relationship with Christ
But you compromise one time too many
Now you sit on the outside looking in
For you didn't keep Christ number one

That's the greatest disease anyone can catch
That disease sends you straight to hell
Oh yes the Savior still loves you
But you can no longer hear his voice

The voice of the Lord is still loud and clear
"Turn back from your wicked ways
And give me first place in your life again
For I still want to be your God

I too, want to walk by your side
So you can stay on the narrow road"
Yet you can't hear the voice of the Lord
The world you embrace, is screaming much lauder

How, oh how, did you get in that place
Where you could no longer hear God's voice
Nor feel the tugging at your hearts door
You embraced Satan's tactic little by little

Now God's still beckoning for you to come
Back into his embrace my friend
But you can't hear the Lord anymore
For Satan has now become your god

You've joined those which make fun of Christians
It's now seven times harder to hear the Lord
For now Satan has your heart for the second time
He sent seven times more to block God

The advice God gives to a believer
Doesn't give place in your life for compromise
When it comes to your salvation
God truly wants the best for your life

Don't allow the disease of Satan
To have any grip on your life
For Satan has only one goal for you
That's to send you straight to hell

Stay totally tuned to the Savior
Reading God's word and praying each day
Asking the Lord to keep you covered with his blood
It's the blood which causes Satan to flee

Never ever cave into political correctness
As our nation is going down the tubes
Without true revival and repentance in man's heart
Our nation is about to fall

Our nation has let its guard down too long
And the churches have sit back and watched
Let's repent and get back to our first love
That's putting Christ at the head of our nation

Every other god can speak out in this nation
But never speak the powerful name of Jesus
Knowing peace can only come through His name
Yet we've embraced the gods of this world

The end of time is rapidly approaching
Are you serving Christ with your whole heart?
Or are you one which has caught the disease
Of compromising, and headed straight to hell

Compromising is not a disease to catch
And be found there, when Jesus comes
Back to earth to receive those
Which will live in heaven with him

If the disease of sin, has you in bondage
My friend you will be left behind
To be tormented for all eternity
Won't you except Jesus into your heart, and be set free

God is beckoning for your call
Ask Jesus to forgive you of all your sins
And if you truly mean it from your heart
You'll be accepted as a child of the King

The old things of sin in your life
Will be totally wiped away
He'll never bring them up again
So your life will begin a new

Turning from your old life
Embracing Jesus in all that you do
You'll never regret making the change
And you'll have a glorious hereafter

Written On: 9-23-13

LOVE

Love, people look at it in different ways
There confused what the word really means
For the world has come into the picture
And they have totally changed it

Most people think love is
What they can accumulate in their life
Which other people have given to them
The more they get the greater the love

Moms and dads give their children
Everything in which they want
And they want their children to have more
Than what they had in their life

Yet look at all of those children
Which were given everything
Without ever having to lift a hand
Most have little appreciation for mom and dad

For when their money runs out
And they can't get what they want
They become bitter in their heart
To the parent which gave them everything

They say their parents don't love them
They think money just grows on trees
And they can keep getting more
In the same place they got it before

Many of these children get into
Drugs, alcohol, and sexual desires
They've been looking in the wrong places
For true love they've been looking for

Because the parent has failed to give
Them the love which they had longed for
They search for things Satan supplies
In the form of the love of man

But the love he pours out to them
Is a false love which never lasts
It takes them deeper down in sin
Once they get there, many are hooked

Like having sex outside of marriage
With the handsome boy in their class
Yet all he's doing is using you
To have sex with as many girls as he can

Now you end up getting pregnant
He has no desire to marry you
He forces you to have an abortion
And to keep your mouth shut to your parents

After the abortion you have more problems
You can't forget the child which you carried
You know abortion is a sin
So it plagues you throughout your life

The boy moves on with his life
Having sex with many more girls
He brags to his friends, of all of the girls
He had sex with, and how proud he was

But a couple of the girls wouldn't abort
The child they now have in their womb
Now he must pay support for the child
Until the child becomes eighteen

They thought sex was called love
They now have bitterness in their heart
Wondering how they got that way
It was because of defying God word

No, love doesn't have anything to do with
Things we do to please ourselves
Love is a relationship
With the Lord Jesus Christ

Love for the Lord is a sacred thing
It's a bonding between you and the Lord
It's a powerful force in our lives
If we embrace Jesus with our whole heart

Loving God will take you to places
Where you never dreamed you would ever go
But the places in which God takes you
Will be a joy and very pleasant to you

Oh yes the Lord may take us
To a whipping post once in a while
For we have started to waver
From the love of God we have embraced

But we'll thank him for taking us to
Different whipping posts along the way
For it takes us to higher heights in Christ
Causing us to love Him greater everyday

Yes Christ knows when we need correction
He'll never shame us along the way
But he'll correct us in different ways
Never to shame us, if we truly love Christ

His correction is to build us up
To do mightier things for him
So as a believer you'll never take offense
To God correcting you in Love

If another believer gets in the flesh
Just push their comments aside
Reject the things they speak to you
But have no bitterness boxed up in you

For if that bitterness gets control
You're the one which will fail
Yet don't be afraid to show them
How their wrong in God's Holy word

Bitterness is like a cancer
If not treated in the first stags
Once it gets total control of you
It will bring death to your life

Remember, bitterness comes from Satan
And when it has total control of you
It can take you to far off places
Destroying your walk with the Lord

We're not here to please man on this earth
But to please the Lord in all we do
So we can have peace in our soul
If we follow God's Holy plan

There are two plans to follow
Satan and the Lord Jesus Christ
There's no living on the fence
That's where Satan wants you to live

Living on the fence, God warns us
That you're neither cold nor hot
He'll spew you out of his mouth
For you can't decide who to live for

Loving the things of this world
Takes your mind off the Savior above
The things you accumulate in this world
Only satisfies for a little while

Like a person which made their first million
They're not satisfied when they arrive there
Now they aim to make a billion
Which consumes their time to get there

Time is so important in our lives
What are we using our time for?
Are we building treasures on this earth?
Which we can't take with us when we die

What good does all the trophies you've got
On the shelf collecting all that dust
Do for you when this life ends
When your trophies are thrown in the trash

But a child of God that loves Jesus
Embracing Him in all that he does
The money you make is to win the lost
So, others will make it to heaven

Then other souls you can take with you
Many souls if you honor the Lord
You might not think you've reached anyone
But you gave, so others could go

Some people you helped go to bible school
Others you sent to the mission field
Many came to know the Savior
Because you gave, with no strings attached

You search the people out you supported
Knowing they love Christ with their whole heart
When you sent them, many came to the Savior
Their souls are also your souls

Once your life on earth comes to an end
The souls they pointed to Christ are also yours
How do I know? God's word tells us that
Some plant, others water, but God gives the increase

So once you learn what love truly is
It's loving people enough to keep them from Hell
Love will have a much greater meaning
Causing you to always want to do more

Do more to point others to the Cross
So they can know what love is about
Then when life on earth is over
God will welcome you into heaven

Your welcoming will be a joyous time
Not having to be ashamed to meet the Lord
Yes meeting the King of Kings, and Lord of Lords
Will be pleasant for you to behold

When God will reach down from his throne
And take your hand, and say welcome home
Then He'll tell you to look behind you
Saying all those people you were responsible for

Yes multitudes were following you
You weren't ashamed to tell others of Christ
And you weren't selfish in your giving
Even if you didn't have much for the Lord

But you gave out of a heart of love
Knowing things weren't important to you
But souls, you desired to see them
Reach heaven know matter the cost

You had a love and compassion for souls
The Lord was number one in your life
Everyone can be a soul winner
But it takes obedience on our part

So the choice is totally in your hands
Will you build treasures on this earth?
Or will you build treasures in heaven
Which moths and rust cannot destroy?

Written On: 7-14-14

JESUS WALKS ON WATER
MATH.14: 22

Have you ever heard the story
Of how Jesus walked on water
So much can be said about it
Which can help us along in life

Yes Jesus proved himself on earth
As he lived his life each day
Knowing he must make the best of each day
His life was planned out for three and half years

Jesus starts out teaching us a truth
Don't just live day by day
But set goals for yourself to reach
And ask the Lord to lead the way

Always remembering one thing my friend
Make sure your plans measure up with God's word
That's the perfect plan God wants us to have
For he wants the best for our life

No, walking each day on water
Isn't the plan God's set for us
Yet you may feel your walking on water
When you live very close to Christ

Christ will take you through many things
To places you wouldn't think you could go
But always remember His Holy Word
"I can do all things through Christ"

No God will never put us on a pedestal
Where we now think we're better than others
For we would then have pride in our life
For pride only comes from the devil

Jesus walked out on the water
After healing many on the shore
He sent the disciples away in a boat
In order to relax from the crowd

But Jesus' plans were much bigger
As he went to the mountain of prayer
To show us we must spend much time
In a quiet place speaking to the Father

You see Jesus knew the storm would rage
It was to teach a truth to the disciples and us
That we can't let fear dominate our life
We need to let Jesus lead the way

He wanted to teach that peace can come
Even in the midst of a storm
Because he is the Prince of Peace
He's always standing by our side

Yes Jesus walked on the water
While the storm was raging so much
Allowing the disciples to see
That in Christ we can have total rest

When the disciple saw him on the water
They thought he was a ghost
But he spoke peace to their hearts
"I'm Jesus, be not afraid"

Peter said "if it be you Lord
Won't you allow me, come to you
By walking on the water
So I know that you are God"

Jesus bid Peter to come
And to keep his eyes focused on him
He began walking on the water
As long as he kept focused on Jesus

But something dreadful happened
He placed his eyes on the storm
Then he began to sink
And he cried out, "Jesus save me"

How often as we live today
We go through storms in our lives
We're not out on the water
We face dreadful storms in our life

Yes, we're a follower of Christ
But the storm seems to over whelm us
We focus on the storm before us
Rather than the one that can calm the storm

The storm we face could be cancer
Or a wayward child which disgraced your life
You lose all of your senses
For you are overwhelmed by them

Jesus is saying keep your eyes on me
Rather than the storm you're going through
For if you focus on me my child
The storm will be short lived

I've allowed the storm to come your way
For I have greater plans for you
The storm you're going through my friend
Is to take you to higher heights

Yes you may have fear, come to your life
In that storm won't you reach out to me
And I will reach back to you
Then we'll walk through the storm together

Stop trying to live your life each day
In your own strength my friend
There are much greater things for you to do
But you first must pass the test

Once you pass the test you'll see
How you'll be used to help many others
You'll be a great asset in the kingdom of God
For I have greater plans for you

So don't hold back in getting all
That I have planned for your life
Yes I'll always be by your side
Hold on to me, and you'll be truly blessed

Written On: 10-10-13

JESUS STARTED AT THE BOTTOM

This might seem so strange to you
As you read the title of this message
But won't you stick with me my friend
So you can understand

Yes Jesus was from the very beginning
But at a point he came to this earth
Jesus was shrunk to micro size
Then was placed in the womb of Mary

Nine months later Christ was born
Yes Christ was God and man
He came to earth to live like man
Giving us direction on how were to live

Mary loved her son so much
And Christ's step father love him so
Not much was told about him
For the first thirty years of his life

The bible tells us about Christ's birth
It was so important for us to know
For Christ's birth was prophesied
Some hundreds of years before

It was prophesied that Christ
Would be born in Bethlehem
Man could never predict such a thing
Yes, hundreds of years before

The prophesy even got more specific
He was to be born in a stable
Then he was to be wrapped in swaddling cloths
It happened just as told years before

Jesus came as one of the most lowly
Not a big announcement when he had arrived
Other than God sent shepherds, and Wiseman
As another proof that Jesus had truly come

Then Jesus lived his early years
Just like you and I did
He worked in the workshop with Joseph
His step dad, which taught him so much

Shortly after Jesus was born
An angel spoke to Joseph to leave
To go to Egypt and stay there
Until he was given word to come back

When the three kings didn't return, Herod
Became wroth and had all children killed
Yes children two years and under
So Jesus wouldn't have a chance to live

That was another prophecy spoken
By Jeremiah the prophet saying
There was heard lamentation and weeping
And great weeping for Rachel's children

There was no comfort for them
Because their children were no more
Herod was such a wicked man
This he did, for he feared the Lord

At the age of twelve Joseph and Mary
Took Jesus to the feast of Passover
And after fulfilling the days
They started home with the group of people

After a day's journey, they realized, Jesus was missing
So when they found him not, they returned
After three days they found him in the temple
Sitting in the temple talking to doctors

He was not just listening to them
But they were asking him questions
Which when Mary and Joseph heard him
They were amazed at how he responded

They told Jesus they had been hunting him
And they were sorrowful because of him
He said, "Why is it ye have sought me
For I must be about my Father's business?"

He left with them, Mary and Joseph
They didn't understand, what he said to them
But his mother kept all these things in her heart
He was subject to them for thirty years

Then at thirty years he stepped out on the scene
It was now time to expose himself
Knowing he must go to the cross
There was much he must do in three years

He picked twelve disciples
When he beckoned for them to come
To be disciples of men
Each obediently came with him

They didn't carry cloths, or food with them
They were told to come just as they were
They obediently followed the Master
From town to town without complaining

Jesus preformed many miracles
He turned water into wine
He healed people wherever he went
And feed five thousand plus women and children

He raised Lazarus from the tomb
After he had been dead three days
That meant that he now stunk
He called out Lazarus, come forth

He didn't yell out, "Come forth"
For everyone in the graves would have risen
His mission was to teach his disciples
Greater things they would do when he left

While Jesus was here on earth
His life was a teaching, for us today
He said that after he was gone
We, which are Christians, will do greater things

Jesus taught us to not give up
For when we go through those trials
It will bring us out so much stronger
Will receive greater things in our life

If we give up when things get tough
We will probably miss the greatest blessing
In which we could ever have
In our lives in which we live

Trials are not a punishment
But a blessing to make us stronger
God sees what we will face in life
And he's preparing us for a greater test

Big tests are such a hard task
If we've failed in the much smaller ones
So face the test head on
Asking the Lord to lead the way

You'll be so glad you didn't give up
And you'll understand the word much more
For tests are made to lift, or build us up
Never to tear us down

When Jesus finally went to the cross
His way to the cross, was not in vain
For many they thought it was over
Yet in three days he came forth from the grave

Jesus showed to us, they can kill the body
Yet they cannot kill the soul
And for each of us that live today
We can face whatever stands in the way

As long as we yield our life to Christ
He'll be with us in all we go through
So don't give up at the toughest times
There's something greater awaiting you

So accept Christ into your life today
Then don't play around with your soul
But leave the Lord, lead the way
He has something special for you

Then when your life finally comes to an end
Christ will be waiting with outstretched arms
To receive you into his kingdom
Saying "welcome home, you've run well

The tests that were placed before you
You ran the race without giving up
So enjoy eternity with me
And all, which have never given up"

For those which never ran the race well
That gave up yielding to the devil
Eternity with Satan will be a long time
Never ever to have peace in your heart

Jesus showed us we can start at the bottom
Yet end up in the palace on the hill
So won't you be found faithful?
What joy when you arrive in heaven

Written On: 5-23-14

CRUCIFIXION

As we take a look at Jesus
The life in which he lived
Here upon this earth
He lived it pure of sin

He had no sin in his life
Christ did nothing but good
He raised the dead, healed the sick
And he even fed five thousand

He showed people how to live
In peace upon this earth
How to love everybody
No matter where they lived

Color meant nothing to him
He loves red, white, and black
You see Jesus does not see color
He sees a person which needs Christ

Even though Jesus did nothing wrong
There was that group of people
Which hated what he taught
Because he said he was the Son of God

They made up things against him
They wanted to move him out of the way
For they saw all those people
Which became followers of Him

They feared he would set up his kingdom
Yes take over their cities and towns
Yes he was the King of Kings
But he wouldn't set up his kingdom on earth

Because of the lies they told
They crucified the King of Kings
Not realizing it was prophesied
Way back in the Old Testament

They beat him with thirty nine stripes
Not realizing it was prophesied it would happen
The thirty nine strips he took
He said by his stripes we are healed

The same happened when they pierced his side
And the blood came running out
His blood covers all our sins
But we must accept him in our heart

They nailed him to the old rugged cross
With a thief on each side
Jesus wanted to show each of us
He died for everyone on earth

The same was offered to each thief
They each had to make a choice
One asked Jesus to forgive him
Jesus said he would be with him in paradise

The other thief saw things differently
He cursed him for not getting him down
So there was no hope for him
Yes he ended up in hell

Both thieves had the same opportunity
For all their sins to be wiped away
What a shame it is for many today
They make the very same mistake

They defy the choice to follow Christ
That's the reason Christ went to the cross
Paid the death no one else could do
To cleanse the whole world from sin

They thought Jesus was gone forever
When they placed him in the tomb
They sealed the tomb very tightly
By rolling that heavy stone in front of it

Then they placed guards in front
Twenty four hours a day
For he claimed that on the third day
He would rise from the grave

His life was fulfilling prophecy
Throughout his life on earth
Why would you expect any different
That on the third day he would rise again

He rose on the third day
Death couldn't hold him in the grave
For remember he is God
He followed through as to what he said

He has been lied about throughout life
That someone stole his body away
But that would be impossible
Because of all the protection which they had

He was seen by many people
Then he ascended back to heaven
To prepare a place for you and me
At the marriage supper of the Lamb

The question each must ask ourselves
Have I surrendered all to Christ?
It's the only way to get to heaven
That's by the man called Jesus Christ

He said many would try other ways
Just like a thief in the night
But when your life is over here below
You'll be sent straight to hell

So won't you make the right choice today?
Surrender your whole life to Christ
Tomorrow may be too late for you
For we don't know when death will come

Written On: 3-28-13

ARE PASTORS PREACHING SALVATION?

So many pastors which call themselves Christian
Preach that you must be born again
Yet it's a very watered down version
To what the bible tells us it is

If all these people which are being reported
Had truly prayed the sinners prayer
Giving their total heart to Jesus
Wouldn't this world be a much better place?

But people pray the sinner's prayer
Then the pastor tells them, their now saved
Yet when they leave the doors of the church
You never see them in the church again

These preachers which head up these churches
Love bragging about all the souls they've saved
The bible tells us that it's only Christ
Which can save a soul from sin

They have told all these people, they are saved
When they left the church that day
But when you approach the pastor later
When their sinning as they did before

They'll quickly answer you
They weren't saved in the first place
When they were the very preacher
Which told them they were saved

So you which are preachers
Stop trying to save people
Start preaching the word of God
And let the word do the convicting

When we do it God's way
And start being concerned about people's soul
Rather than being more concerned about numbers
Will start seeing souls flooding to our alters

Their more concerned about numbers
Than to truly see people's lives changed
For to many a soul is molded
To send them straight to Hell

Satan must be sitting back and laughing
At the mentality of so called Christians today
Satan knows that if you believe them
His coffers in Hell will be full

Yes Satan is a deceiver
He has blinders on so many in the pulpit
Which then flows right to the pew
It's the church which has failed in the world

Oh yes, the banner of Christ is still strong
Yet so many don't embrace the Lord above
For they want their ears tickled
They can then feel good and sin all they want

Yes, just take a week at a time
Getting through the problems you face
"I'll only search for what I want
And not give Christ total control of my life"

Our churches are filled with so many programs
Which have no power to lead people to Christ
They only help to ease the mind
To make us feel good for another week

We talk to everyone about the programs
Not about what Christ has done for me
So people think all the church is for
Is to have fun and keep living as before

Because of how the churches present Christ
Not wanting anyone to get upset
We're creating people that don't know Christ
Other than that Christ is a very good man

What we fail to realize
God loves everyone on earth
But God doesn't see love as we do
Many times discipline is love

You might say what do you mean?
Just think of it this way
Kids which are never corrected
Will seldom turn out all right

Your children will become disobedient
Disrespectful to everyone they meet
For rules are never applied
To that child you're raising up

That's how so many churches are being run
All their doing is pleasing people
So people are going to Hell every day
And these people don't know where there headed

We have gotten so far from what Christ
Wants the church to be on this earth
God wants us to preach the whole truth
Not to pick and choose what we want

It's time we stop making Christians
By standards which we set
It just makes things so much easier
For we mold people to think as we do

But it's time to get back to the Bible
Letting the Holy Spirit lead your life
Yes, it's time we start getting serious
To serve the Lord with our whole heart

It's time we start telling people
To pray the sinners prayer
But only if Christ is convicting them
For they can't do it on their own

Then tell them, the only way they can be saved
Is they must surrender everything to Christ
Then they must turn from there old ways
Repenting of all the wrongs they've done

For so many, not a tear is ever shed
For their not planning to live for Christ
Their only trying to please you
So you can have another person to brag about

It's time we get back to God's principles
Teaching the whole truth of God's word
Preaching that they are headed to Hell
If they don't turn their whole life over to Christ

Teaching them, it's so much more then saying
The sinners prayer while at the alter
Yes we must repent of the past life we've lived
Then there's another step we must take

That step is turning from our old ways
Leaving the old ways at the alter
Then start studying the Bible everyday
And each day spend much time in prayer

If you don't have that desire to serve Christ
You can say the sinner's prayer all you want
But you'll still be headed to the pit of Hell
Never ever to have peace and rest

Repentance is the most important thing
Not salvation, as so many want you to believe,
For too many people throw that word out
Then people everywhere say their saved

So let's get back to the word of God
What does the Bible say about it
It says we must repent of our past life
Turning to the new life in Christ

We can go through all the hoops
Many churches are portraying today
Without repenting and turning from your old ways
You won't have Jesus in your heart

Our life must reflect the life of Christ
Old self will take a back step
Yes the more we take on the life of Christ
The more of self will fade away

It's then people which we meet each day
Will start desiring what we have
For anytime we reflect Jesus
Old Satan will have to flee

The question only we can answer
Has my life been totally changed?
Where I reflect more of Jesus everyday
It's only then, the world won't control your life

Many people will bring up that scripture
In Math. 7:20 on how we will know them
"By their fruits you will know them"
But remember to interpret scripture with scripture

But remember so many preachers
Put most everyone into heaven
When they preach the funerals
Of many which their lives are questionable

So why not leave it up to the Lord
Maybe saying, you pray everything was all right
With their soul then leave it there, and then you won't
Be held accountable if they don't make it to heaven

But a person can know if their going
By asking yourself these questions
Yes by answering them honestly
Rather than trying to deceive yourself

The questions is what or who
Do I spend the most time with?
I spend more time with the Savior
And less time with the world?

Who or what am I investing in?
Is it things which make me feel good?
Yes, things which others measure you with
By all the things which you accumulate

Or have I been investing in heavenly things
Yes your money to win souls for Christ
So your life will be a light on the hill
Christ will then be flowing through you

So let's stop following preachers
We follow them only, if their following Christ
We determine it by studying God's word
To prove what their saying is right

You have a choice to make
Will I serve self or the Lord
Serving Christ will give you a joyous life
And assuring you a place in heaven

Written On: 2-11-15

WHY

How many times throughout the day
Do you hear the word why?
Is the word appropriate to say?
It's only you that can make the right choice

We say why, to so many things
Why do I have to go to school?
All because you don't want to go
You ask the question, Why?

How often do you hear these words
When you wake up on Sunday morn
Why do I have to go to church?
There are other things I want to do

If the Lord isn't embedded in your soul
It's a task to get ready for church
For the love of Jesus isn't embedded
Deep down into your soul

The world has control of you
So you're longing to serve self
Yes the things you want to do
Rather than follow the way of the Lord

The question is, why don't you
Serve the Lord which created you
And everything in this world
To satisfy the longing of your soul?

The one which has your best at heart
He sent the Holy Spirit to nudge your soul
Warning that you're headed, down the wrong road
But he'll not force himself on anyone

He gave unto every one of us
A choice to choose either right or wrong
Too many are making bad choices
Not realizing until it's too late

The reason their making bad choices
Their living their life for self
Then they look back over their life saying
Why Lord, did you allow me to make that choice?

But it wasn't the Lord that made that choice
It was your will to choose what you wanted
It's important to make the right choices
That's why it's better to let the Lord, lead the way

We question, "Why Lord do you write
Those passages in your Holy book?
But the choice is so plain to see
God wants you to flee from them

We weren't placed upon this earth
To live each day for ourselves
We were placed to serve the Lord
To please him in all that we do

He knows when you learn to put Christ first
Your life will be renewed and refreshed
Then you will start saying these words
Why didn't I turn to the Lord sooner?

The Lord always has your best at heart
He'll lead you through the still waters
Which brings to you, life, peace, and joy
Which calms all phases of your life

Jesus desires to bring peace to your soul
In order to help you make the right choices
Then you'll not be ashamed of the choices you made
The choices you made were proper for you

Anytime you regret things you do
You're living your own desires
You weren't living close to the Cross
But trying to live too close to the edge

Be assured if you're living to close to the edge
In order to get things you want
Knowing the things your doing are questionable
You will not make it to heaven

Why don't you change your mentality
Saying "What Lord, would you have me do?"
Be assured the Lord will give you the answer
If you're truly serious in your heart

Sometimes the answer comes through a person
He sends your way for you
It comes at that very moment
Before you make the wrong choice

That's a red flag for you
To make the right choice
Yet many fail to hear what they say
For that day you failed to pray

Sometimes you get the answer
As you read the Bible each day
Saying "Lord, will you give me your will?"
Which will be the very word I need

Sometimes he probes people's hearts
As they pray to God each day
Sometimes he'll answer when you go to bed
He comes to you in the form of a dream

No matter how he may answer
You'll not hear him if you're not listening
For Christ to answer your prayers
That's how most people live each day

So stop always asking why
But expect him to answer your prayer
Be assured the answer will come to you
Sometimes through the oddest ways

    Written On: 7- 22-14

WHO WILL BE IN HEAVEN?

Most people don't want to talk about
Who will be in the place called Heaven?
They just know they won't make it there
They just believe it will fade away

Yet Hell is a real place
God made it for Satan and his angles
Yet since Adam and Eve fell in the garden
Those which don't follow Christ will go there

God had no intention for it to happen
Yet when Adam and Eve sinned
It was they which changed God's plan
For every man, woman, and person on earth

Today everyone is born in sin
Yet there is a short time you are exempt
It's that time when you aren't accountable
In your life as a child

The time varies for each child
It varies to how you're exposed to the word
Some which are exposed to the gospel early
Their accountability time will start sooner

Probably the latest day for a child
Is somewhere around the age of twelve
That's the time when the Jewish people
Have the bar mitzvah for their sons

After the unaccountability time is over
There are then many which will go to Hell
You might be curious who they are
Let's take a look at many of them

Selfish people won't make it to heaven
Yes they'll end up in Hell
For it's all about themselves
Not thinking about the Lord Jesus Christ

Unthankful is another group
Of people which will end up there
For they don't appreciate anything
They only think about themselves

Self-righteous people are another group
Of people which will be in Hell
They talk about all the things they do
Feeling their better than everyone else

We find people like this in every phase of life
And the worst place we can find them
Is in the church which God designed
Where people's needs are to be met

So many have made the church a circus
A place to ramp and rage, of what they have done
Not sharing what Christ has done for them
It's all about our own self righteousness

We want to be in the spot light
And if we don't get what we want
Bless God I'll not stay at that church
I'll find a church where I can steal the show

That's because their only living for themselves
Nothing else matters to them
That's exactly where Satan wants them
For he has them on the road to Hell

Do-Gooders are another group
Of people which are headed to Hell
For no one can do things like them
So they'll put down everyone else

No one can do it as they do
So no one had better get in there way
For bless God I'm the only one
That can do the job well

Thieves and robbers are another group
Of people which are headed to Hell
For they only want what others have
And bless God I'll not work for it

People with unforgiveness in there heart
These type people are everywhere
Yes they are strung around the world
So many are in our churches

That's why congregations have so many problems
Unforgiveness is embedded in their soul
They say all things are alright with them
Yet their holding unforgiveness in their heart

How many people, have left the Church
Most people shouldn't have left it
They left the church for another one
Because they had bitterness towards others

That bitterness was embedded deep within
Sometimes even forgetting they have it
But God above is keeping records
Of all the bitterness you hold inside you

There are certain people which you once loved
Now you stay your distance from them
For bless God they did something to me
And I cannot forgive them

If you're not willing to forgive these people
You're just as bad as they are
And if you don't truly forgive them
You'll end up in the pit of hell

Those which were once pillars in the church,
Which loved the Lord with all their heart,
Yet something drastic happened in the church
Maybe between you and another

So now you're sitting on the outside
Of the church you once attended
And won't even enter another church
For your holding bitterness inside your heat

You think you're only holding it against others
But you're holding it deep inside you
Also at the one which can help you
Yes, you're holding that bitterness towards God

Now you let other things control your life
Even surrounding yourself with family and friends
Yes you're doing all types of good things
Which makes you feel real good

Those good things are sent your way
To make you feel good inside
Yet those good things control your life
Pushing the Savior farther from you

Yes Satan loves you doing those good things
Just don't have a personal relationship with Christ
If he keeps you long enough
He'll see you in the pit of Hell

How often are you being deceived?
Doing things you should not do?
This deceiving is sent to you by Satan
To send you to the pit of Hell

We're deceived that we don't have to
Go to church each week of our life
But God set the church in order
For us to go each week to be blessed

It's there our soul is filled with spiritual food
And we're to be obedient to the Lord
To bring our tithes to the church each week
We don't have a choice to give or not

The tithes show our obedience to Christ
It's our means to show Christ we love him
That I'll be obedient to you dear Lord
And I'll not put a stipulation on it

That's different than when the plate passes by
You hold back in what God requires of you
Yes the ten percent is required of you
And sometimes you give with a grudging heart

When giving with a grudging heart
It's just like not giving at all
For God cannot bless a person my friend
Without giving because you love Him

These are things which will send you to Hell
Most people are going to Hell every day
Unless you have surrendered all to Christ
Then turned from your old life you've lived

You must take on the new life of Christ
Desiring to do all he wants you to do
Don't look back to what you once did
For looking back can take you off track

You can't live on your past experiences
With the Savior, up in heaven above
Or you can't get to heaven on your parents merits
As many in this world want you to believe

Everyone will stand before the Lord
Telling the Lord what they have done
You must keep your life up to date
Until you take your last breathe on earth

God will have to say to you
Depart from me I never knew you
For your name isn't in my book
No your name isn't written there

You might say, how can that ever be
I once surrendered my life to Christ
But you failed in your daily walk with Christ
You started compromising your life with the world

You stopped producing fruit for the Lord
So at a point Christ will cut you off
He'll sever you from the vine Jesus Christ
Never to be connected again

For once you're severed from the vine
You then die to the things of Christ
Now it is all about yourself
You'll now hold bitterness towards Jesus Christ

You might say, how can that be?
Once you have been born again
The way you get connected to the vine
Is by accepting Jesus into your heart

But you squandered your life away
Playing around with the things of the world
Not always playing around with bad things
But things which take us from following Christ

So that is a bad place to be in
For you never have a chance to enter Heaven
For you have wasted away your day of grace
The Lord can no longer get to your heart

So if you should find yourself drifting
You need to quickly turn from that life
Repent of the sins you have committed
Before the sins over take you

The Bible tells us all have sinned
And come short of the glory of God
That there is none righteous
No not one, no not one

Then it tells us in Romans 6:23
That the wages of sin is death
What that's saying to each of us
That everyone is headed to Hell

But Jesus did something special for us
He died, was buried, and rose again
He did that for you and me
It's the only way for us to be set free

So the 23rd verse didn't stop there
Christ had us all on his mind
So the gift of God is eternal life
Through Jesus Christ our Lord

Jesus didn't go to Calvary in vain
He made the choice to set man free
No He didn't have to go there
He loved man kind to much to not go

So if you don't want to go to Hell
It's time to surrender to Christ right now
Tomorrow may be one day to late
Because death or the rapture may take place

Be assured you're not taking the chance
To have a great hereafter
Eternity lasts forever my friend
The choice is up to you, will it be Heaven or Hell?

Written On: 5-26-15

WHO IS A DISCIPLE?

A disciple is a believer in Christ
They've become a follower of Him
They follow him each step they take
As he teaches them to search their heart

When the Savior speaks to their soul
Their quick to repent of the things
Which their soul has been quickened about
There quick to turn from that sin

But wait, there are some which become relaxed
And they start thinking about their past
They start questioning the life they live
And over time they lose out with Christ

You may say, Christians can't lose out
The question is does God's word lie?
Turn to John 6:60 thru verse 71
And God's word tells us many disciples fell away

They no longer embrace the love of Christ
For they didn't agree in what God was teaching
After following Christ for many years
Jesus said some of you believe not

Then as we study the parable
About the true vine which is Jesus Christ
Yes Jesus is the true vine
And God is Lord of all

He teaches us in this parable
We're to stay connected to the vine
He's speaking to believers
And not speaking to the world

How do I know he's speaking to believers?
He tells us were connected to the vine
We have accepted Christ as our Savior
We've began the journey walking with Christ

But somewhere along the way
We've become relaxed in our walk with Christ
Giving Satan room to speak softly to us
Then we start compromising our Christian walk
As we start compromising
Things on the outside start looking good
You now think they're not so bad
So you accept the trivial things Satan shares

God's word says Satan's a deceiver
He'll start working on your life
The things aren't bad within them self
Yet they weaken your walk with Christ

Things which take up your time each day
Where we don't have time for the Lord
Our prayer and our studying time
Are pushed back until another time

But time seems to never come
So you're quickly drifting in your walk with Christ
Now you're not producing for the Lord
For the world has your life and not Christ

Christ has tried pruning you many times
By knocking at your hearts door
Or sending another believer to speak to you
But you quickly push them aside

You told that other believer
Everything was alright in your soul
Knowing that down deep in your heart
You lied, but you want them off your back

After many proddings at your heart
You refuse to give into the Holy Spirit
And finally the Lord, cuts you off
For you know longer are producing for Christ

Helping others find the love of Christ
No longer takes priority in your life
You can't hear God probing at your heart
For Satan is now soothing your soul

You're enjoying all that this world provides
Yes you've now caved into pleasing yourself
So now it's what I desire
And not what God desires for my life

Once God severs you from the vine
You're now like a rose cut from its branch
Once it's been cut off
It will soon wither and die

Our lives are like that rose
Once we've been severed from the Lord
We now embrace the things of this world
And there's no desire for the things of Christ

So if you find yourself drifting
Don't put it off another day
To ask Christ to forgive you
And accept you back into his fold

For if you drift too far
God will eventually cut you off
Don't allow yourself to get there
For your only alternative then, is Hell

Written On: 11-4-13

WHO ARE YOU FOLLOWING?

People all around the world
Are following someone or something
But is that something which you're following
Bringing glory to the King of Kings

Many of our churches are filled
But who are they filled with
Are they filled with individuals?
Who don't glorify the Lord Jesus Christ?

I'm afraid so many in our churches
Are there with just a form
Yes a form of worship to the Lord
But the form is to please themselves

All they are concerned about
Is feeling real good
So they can go out in the world
Bragging of the big congregation they go to

It's all about what I do
Maybe you're a teacher, or a preacher
Or that you sing in the big choir
Even head up the men's or woman's group

People are looking up to you
So it makes you feel real good
Yet you spend little time in prayer
And yes, less time in God's Word

Oh you're one which has decided
To learn many passages in which you quote
Yet you fail to apply the Word
To your life you live each day

It's all about what I do
You even say that you're a Christian
For you went to the alter
Some fifty years before

You've learned to say the right words
Yes you've learned to manipulate people
To get them to do things
Which make you feel real good

You have what you call power
But God calls what you do
Nothing but a foolish man
Which won't get you to heaven

You may say how foolish you are
To say such a thing about him
But you see he's only religious
God says they will not make it to heaven

All the things in which you're doing
Are all good within themselves
They make man feel real good
Yes they get involved in the church

But it's all about works
It takes more than works to please the Lord
For works are really good things
But they alone will lead you straight to Hell

Real works come after you make a commitment
To the Lord of Lord, and King of King
Yes you must first accept Christ into your heart
Then turn from the past life you lived

When you went to the alter before
And repeated the sinners prayer
You weren't serious in your heart
To give Jesus your whole heart and life

So now you are deceiving people
And people are following you
So not only will you end up in Hell
But those you're teaching to be like you

But if you should surrender your heart to Christ
God will renew you through and through
Your life will change from pleasing yourself
To pleasing the Lord Jesus Christ

Then good works will come to you
You'll study God's word each day
Applying the truth to your life
For it's now about pleasing the Lord

There's probably eighty percent in the churches
Which are headed to the pit of Hell
For them, it's all about works
Just trying to please the congregation

But God is calling out to you
I love all the good things you're doing
But the only way to enter heaven
Is through the blood of my perfect Son

Yes I sent Him to this earth to die
Upon that old rugged cross
He died, was buried, and rose again
On the third day, which man said couldn't happen

Jesus had a choice he had to make
He didn't have to follow through with it
But Jesus looked down through time
Seeing that we would end up in Hell

Jesus didn't want Satan to have total control
He wanted man to have a choice
So He followed through with God's plan
Jesus chose to do it for you and me

The thing which made it possible
For you and I to be set free
He came forth from the grave
On the third day just like He promised

That made it possible for every person
Yet it does not come automatically
We must accept Christ into our heart
Then turn from the life we once lived

Giving everything to the Lord
Realizing everything already belongs to Him
That we're only given the things we have
To manage them for a while

Then we must stay focused on Christ
No we're not to keep looking back
For when you keep looking back
You'll start dabbling around with the world

Christ has everything you need
Enjoy everything he gives to you
Stop stepping off the path
For that's what Satan wants you to do

He'll put doubt and fear in your heart
Then you'll start acting on them
And if you stay there too long
Christ will have to cut you off

Once you are cut from the vine
The vine being Jesus Christ
You can't never to be attached again
For dead branches have no life

So if you find that you're drifting
Stop and repent of your sins, right now
For the Lord is reaching with arms open wide
To receive you back into the fold

Yes you can lose your salvation
But Jesus doesn't want you to
So repent and stay close to the Cross
Where blessings will continue to flow

If you follow God's plan everyday
Desiring all that Christ has for you
Be assured that Christ is waiting for you
When you leave this life on earth

Written On: 6-7-15

LEPROSY

In the world we live today
We don't hear much about leprosy
There could be two reasons why
Just put your thinking cap on

All of the medical advances they have
They could have wiped leprosy out
Or maybe there are very few of them
And they've given it a modern name

A name which doesn't draw
Attention to that dreadful disease
That's the way the world works today
They love keeping people blind to them

There's a much more serious leprosy
In this old world in which we live
It's not always easily detected
There's a covering over much of it

This leprosy is all around us
There's no way to detect it all
It's hidden everywhere we turn
And believe me, it is intentional

We find it in every bar
And the local grocery store
You can find it in a car lot
Even in the barber shop

It's found in the department stores
And at the mall down town
You can find it in the beauty parlor
And the stores where they fix your nails

You find it in the homes we live
And any event you may go to
You find it at your neighbor's house
Along with all your relatives

There isn't any place you don't find it
It is no respecter of persons
And sad to say you even find it
In all churches around the world

This leprosy is found everywhere
People around you and everyone else
It's no respecter of persons
Respecting whether your rich or not

The leprosy which I'm talking about
Is far worse then what eats the body
For this leprosy which I'm talking about
Pierces deep inside the soul

Then if you don't deal with it my friend
It will totally consume your life
To where all hope, will be gone
And you will end up in hell

What is this leprosy which eats at you
This leprosy is the worst you can get
This leprosy is the kind that doesn't kill the body
But it does kill the soul

That's the Holy Spirit probing your heart
Telling you to turn from your sins
For everyone is a sinner
Until we learn how to deal with it

If we deal with it in Jesus name
That's the only way it can be wiped away
Asking Jesus to come into your heart
An cleanse you from all your sins

If you truly mean it with all your heart
Then turn from your wicked ways
Embracing Jesus, with all your heart
Asking Jesus, to lead the way

Be assured he will not fail you
That's why he beckons you to come
Into his presence giving up the past
So you can have sweet fellowship with him

If you feel that tugging, don't turn him away
It will be the greatest choice you could make
Let this be the greatest day you ever had
By asking Jesus to reign supreme in your life

When people say they're turning a new leaf
I'm going to do something different on my own
But the new leaf they have turned to
Will soon fizzle out for them

But when you take and replace your old life
By going to the foot of the Cross
Remembering what Christ did for you and I
When he was crucified, buried, and rose again

When you embrace him with all you heart
He will quickly embrace you so tightly
And you'll wonder why you waited so long
To embrace the Lord Jesus Christ

If you keep focused on Christ every day
He'll take you to heights you've never known
And the best part of total surrender to him
He'll prepare you a place in heaven

Oh yes you will stumble along the way
But keep your focus on Christ
And quickly ask him to forgive you
Of whatever sin you've committed

Those stumbling blocks that come to you
Doesn't mean Christ know longer loves you
But when that trial comes to your life
If you stay focused on Christ

You'll come out stronger then you were before
That's why trials come your way
To help us grow stronger every day
Then thank the Lord for being with you through them

Then when this life comes to an end
It will be worth the trials you went through
For this life is short compared to eternity
It determines which life you will live

If you don't give Christ your all
He'll not be awaiting you
But if you make Jesus number one
You'll have a wonderful life in heaven

Written On: 12-31-14

SANCTUARY

Oh how precious is that place
Many don't know how precious it is
It was designed by the Lord
It's a place to learn about Him

It was designed as a tabernacle
A place only certain people could go
Then you had the Holy of Holy's
Which only certain priests could enter in

If anyone else entered the Holy of Holy's
They were quickly killed
Not by those on the earth
But they were killed by the Lord

You may say it doesn't happen today
How many sit on the alter
Then talk about everything else but God
When the alter is such a sacred place

We allow our children to carry on
In the sanctuary of the church
When we should honor it
A place we're entering, as a place of the Lord

We as adults are no different
It's a place to get caught up on the past
Not things to uplift the Son of God
But all the things the world offered to them

We will be held accountable
For not honoring the house of God
Maybe not now, but when we meet God
On judgment day my precious friend

How we treat the house of God
Tells to us what type Christian we are
Which if we don't honor the house of God
Will not honor Christ in the world

It's a place spent gossiping
About the neighbor that lives next door
Or someone there in the church
That you do not care about

Then word gets back to each of them
It turns them farther away from Christ
You say that you're a Christian
But God calls you a hypocrite

You spend all your time talking about
All the different sports of the week
You spend so little time in the house of God
We waste away the little time we spend in God's house

All the things you talked about at church
They take priority over the Lord
You say we're not like the tabernacle
It depends what you are talking about

But you're right when you say
The church is not like the tabernacle
Where the Spirit of the Lord fell
And they are bathed in the presence of God

But that's where you are wrong
Christ still meets people there
He still meets people at the alter
For all types of needs you might have

People will pay for how they treat the alter
The church and all its furnishings
Yes, it is still a sacred place today
How are you treating God's house

The Holy Spirit has been replaced
With all the cares of this world
We have watered down the gospel
Mixing it with the world

No, Christ isn't number one in most churches
Things are consuming God's Holy House
So God has been pulling His Holy Spirit back
For we know longer seek His leading

People are dying every day
In the churches which we attend
We try to put everyone in heaven
But God's word teaches other wise

We will be held accountable
For all the souls we send to Hell
What you're not realizing
Is your sending your own self to Hell

We wonder why people aren't flocking
To the doors of the church you attend
The Holy Spirit is no longer welcome
Because your church has become as the world

Some churches are drawing people
By all the programs which they have
But they lift up the world in all they teach
Satan is the only one lifted up

Satan has deceived the church
To where the power of God isn't welcome
So the people are being sent to Hell
One service at a time

You say Hell is a very strong word
But that's exactly what is happening
The church is no different than the world
People which once served Christ are losing out

Not only are they losing they're salvation
But their dragging multitudes with them
They've made the church lukewarm
Their lives have become the same

Yes the church was once a church
Where the power of the Lord fell
Where people truly found the Lord
And their lives were totally changed

When they left the doors of the church
Sports which once controlled their lives
Was replaced with the love of the Lord
Christ now became the speech they shared

But today most that repeat the sinners prayer
Treat it as nothing more than a ritual
For when they leave the doors of the church
They're no different than when they came in

You think your church has every thing
You want a church to have
But you talk about the church across town
Where the Spirit of the Lord is moving

If your church was so powerful
You wouldn't have to talk about the other churches
But you have begun to notice
That some of your people are sneaking to them

Some of them have found the Savior
Their life has been totally renewed
There pulling people from your church
For the Holy Spirit isn't welcomed in yours

They've found what serving Christ is about
That serving Christ will prepare you for Heaven
They have embraced the Christ of Calvary
The cares of this life know longer dominate them

Christ has now become number one
In their life they live each day
There now making an impact for Jesus
No matter where they may go

Oh yes the other church you came from
Is losing people one after another
For they're not about to change
From the lukewarm person they've become

If you want all Christ has for you
You must cast the world from your life
Making Christ number one in your life
Then people will begin to take notice

Take notice that your desire to reach heaven
Is a serious step in which you've taken
No matter how the world treats you
You're a child of God, and you're going to stay intact

You'll spend much time in the Word
And much time in communication with God
Each day you'll give him your best
In everything in which you do

You'll not do questionable things
Which the world says are alright
But you'll live out the word of God
You know the Lord requires it of you

You will not live close to the edge
Trying to get by with all that you can
But you will excel every day you live
Going the second mile in your walk with Christ

Each must be honest with himself
How is my life measuring up with the Lord's?
Am I doing everything that I can?
To please the Lord when I face Him

Or will the things in which I do each day
Be questionable before the Lord
Don't allow yourself to be ashamed before the Lord
When you meet the Lord on judgment day

Written On: 3-10-13

I WAS RELIGIOUS

I've fought you Lord for many years
I'd been taught these things all my life
That we were to fight to keep things
The same as they've been for years

I didn't realize that many of the teachings
Had no merit in God's word
I just knew what dad and mom had taught me
Along with the church I'd attended for years

The preacher was such a loving person
Each trusted the preacher that he'd teach them well
Nothing but the word of God
So I believed just what the preacher said

At times when we didn't have church
I'd sneak out to other churches
Most were not the same type
That we attended all those years

I listened to many on TV and radio
I was hungering for more of Christ
And some of those preachers said
Don't believe me check me out with God's word

That was something I'd never heard before
Because our preacher thought he was right
And he didn't want others to question him
He was nothing more than a people pleaser

Everyone which backed and loved that preacher
Would never question what the preacher said
They felt if they would defy the preacher
They would be held accountable to the Lord

No, you don't attack the preacher
But it's alright to question things he says
If they don't measure up to the word of God
Yet you never attack to destroy him

If he fails to answer your questions
Pushing them aside as nothing to worry about
If enough of your questions go against the Lord
Just be careful you don't have a bitter heart

It's alright to move to another church
Where you can be fed the things of God's Word
But when you leave that church my friend
Don't make a big show as you leave

Just leave that church on your own
Don't drag others along with you
For if you drag others along with you
You're defying God, and it's a sin

Keep loving all those people
As you meet them on the street
Just set a very good example
Of what living for Christ is about

God may have moved you from that place
It may be between you and the Lord
Because your heart was hungering for more
And you would never receive at that church

God may have moved you from that church
Because he didn't want you to become religious
He saw the great hunger in your heart
By moving you on, you could do more for Christ

Never leave a church if you're being used
To spread the good news of God's word
But when your gift is being stripped away
That's God telling you it's time to move on

But leave the church on a good note
Then keep hungering for more of Christ
Asking the Lord to guide you
To the next appointment for you

Don't take things into your own hands
But be willing to not get in a hurry
Be willing to wait on the Lord
He'll then guide you, to where he wants you to go

Never leave a church so you can hide
Yes hide in the midst of a crowd
Of another church so you can relax
Yes you get lost, so others don't know you're there

For if you don't want work to do
In the next church you attend
You will become lukewarm in your heart
And it could lead you straight to Hell

If you don't know what to do
But you know Christ has sent you there
Ask the pastor what you can do
But first bath your soul in prayer

You don't want to become part of a program
Unless it lifts up the Lord Jesus Christ
Yes, programs may bring people to your church
But many programs send people to Hell

Unless the program teaches them the Word
And is bathed and birthed in prayer
Just being a part of a program
Can teach nothing, but to be a good person

Good people go to Hell every day
For they don't have a relationship with Christ
So don't get caught up in the tricks of Satan
Doing what self wants you to do

Never follow the pastor or preacher
Unless there following the truth of God's word
For many a teacher and preacher
Are only concerned in building a big church

They build their church on popularity
Without the anointing of God in their life
Then they have nothing more than lukewarm people
Which are following the preacher and not the Lord

So stay true to God's Holy Word
Making sure your living for Christ
Not searching for what you want
Instead of depending on the leading of God

Walk each day bathed in prayer
And spend much time in God's word
Always seeking what God has for you
So you'll be on track, with what God has for you

The Lord has a job for each of us
No matter how well or sick you are
He wants you to be a living testimony
Until you take your very last breath

Yes you can live for God in the good, or the bad
For the Lord said he'd walk by your side
He's the only one you can trust in
So stay true to His Holy Word

Won't you commit your life to Christ
Stop following the ways of religion
So you're nothing more than a religious person
With no power, for you don't know Christ

Won't you yield your total life to Jesus
Trusting Him in all that you do
So you'll have a place in heaven
When you take your last breath on earth

Written On: 9-24-13

HOW DO I VIEW OR TREAT THE LORD

There is so much to think about
When it comes to serving the Lord
Who or what God am I serving?
And how do I treat him every waking hour

You wake up in the morning
Grab a cup of coffee and the newspaper
Or flip on the TV set
To get caught up on the latest news

Of course you wait for the sports analyzer
To give play by play all the games of the night before
So you can fit into the crowd
That you'll meet throughout the day

So you can stand up with the best of them
If you're up to date with all the stats
And it will make you feel so good
They'll think I'm the most intelligent man they know

You live your life throughout the day
You think it's the most rewarding day for you
So you finally pat yourself on your back
Then lay down and fall off to sleep

You start dreaming during the night
The Savior starts speaking to your heart
You failed to have communication with me
You left your prayer schedule out of your life

How about your little children
In which you brought into the world
They wanted to speak to their mom or dad
But you were too busy with the world

One day your child will be just like you
Or worse, as they have totally watched you
Your life was being planted deeply
In your children, you brought into the world

They saw that you were selfish
You wanted your way and no one else's
Unless the things others told you
Benefitted no one but yourself

As the Lord came to you in a dream
He said you didn't take time in the Word
When you knew you were to study it
In order to prove that you loved him

So when you talked to people throughout the day
You gave people your own opinion
Which was so far from the truth
You formed your opinion from people and not from the Word

That one which spoke to you that day
Asking you who would get to Heaven
You told them all they had to do
Was pray the sinners prayer and they would be saved

Then you were taught at your local church
That you would always be saved
Yes, that's what the denomination believes
So I'll believe all the scripture they gave

So now you're following the denomination
Rather than to find the truth
Your mind is now warped to pleasing people
Rather than to study God's word for truth

What about the man with the other passages
Which tells that your salvation can be lost
You quickly blank them out of your Bible
Yes you blank them out of your mind

For you liked what the preacher told you
For you will never lose your salvation
Your preacher didn't tell you the whole truth
So you're rapidly heading to Hell

God says "I'm speaking to your heart
For I want you to change direction
Stop accepting what others tell you
That is what Satan wants you to do

Take the passages that teach both ways
Then study each of them very well
For my word does not lie
But you must study to find the truth"

Yes there is an answer my friend
They are each partially right
But they are failing to tell you
That God gave everyone a will

When you understand what a will is
I'll never force myself on any one
Then you'll know, no one can take you from Christ
But only you, for it is your will

God says, "Yes I've sealed you till the day of redemption
But that's only on my part
You can break that seal at any time
But when you do, you'll lose your soul

Oh yes I'll take you to higher heights
But your church or pastor is holding you back
But I want to fill you with my Holy Spirit
So you can climb to higher heights"

But no, your denomination teaches
You receive the Holy Spirit when you believe
And they are one hundred percent right
But there's more to it than at salvation

If you had studied the Holy Scriptures
There is another step you can take
Yet you fail to believe it because
You've been taught, you now have it all

But if you will study God's Holy Word
It says that in the last days you will be filled
With the Holy Spirit with the evidence
Of you speaking with other tongues

But your denomination has told you
That it was only for the church of that day
When the disciples walked this earth
Yet God's word says it will happen in the last days

Yes in order for you to receive this gift
There are different gifts for you to choose from
But it is totally up to you my friend
All gifts are available to each and every one

Just read in the Holy Scriptures
All the gifts which are available to you
Each one is still available today
There's no reason, for you to be afraid

But you must seek them with your whole heart
Giving Christ first place in your life
Then stop living for yourself
And put Christ first place in all you do

You'll learn that you've been stealing from God
For you haven't made Christ number one
You may say, how have I stolen from you
You have failed to pay your tithes

That isn't something for us to decide
It's a command in God's Holy Word
That's why you have so many problems
You fail to be obedient to the Lord

Then you've been taught offerings aren't important
That's nothing more than a trick of Satan
He knows blessings will start pouring out to you
If all is given with no strings attached in love

The Word says, "You receive not, because you ask not
After you have given you whole life to me
I'm here to pour blessings out to you
Yet you fail to be obedient to my word

You want to pick and choose what you want to do
So you're losing out with me each day
For you are living for yourself
And not living for the Lord

Yes I demand in my Holy Word
That you follow in my foot steps
Which I have laid out for you
I know how you can be totally blessed

But no, you are serving other gods
You might think that you're alright
But I am a jealous God
I'll not serve, with any other god

You have deceived so many around you
They all make you feel so good
But you are serving the god of self
An you're so far from pleasing the Lord"

You're at a crossroad in your life
There's a choice you must make
God has spoken, that's why he's visited you now
It could be your last chance you'll have

There's so much I have in store for you
I'll always have your best at heart
But now everything is in your lap
You must choose whom you will serve

My arms are opened real wide
But my book is filled with all your sins
I can wipe them all away
Then you can start all over again

Won't you surrender all to Jesus
And mean it from deep inside your heart
God knows whether you're playing around
Or whether you've given all to Him

So once you wake up from your dream
Won't you surrender all to Christ
And He'll cover all your sins with His blood
Never to remember them again

Written On: 4-5-14

HOW ARE YOU WALKING?

So many walk their walk each day
Not knowing where they want to go
For they haven't made up their mind
Just what direction is best for them

They say that they're a Christian
Yet their life is so confused
They have not made up their mind
Whether to live for Christ or not

They say that they serve God
That's how Satan has us confused
For anyone can serve a god
This world is full of them

They all live in the shadow of the cross
The cross means little to them
That gives you a choice of god's
Yes, as many as you desire to worship

God has become a passive word
Even in the churches which we attend
All because we live in the shadow
Yes the shadow of the cross

When you live in the shadow
You only learn to pretend
That the shadow is for real
The shadow is cast over you

That's why most people in the pew
Only want a little bit each Sunday
Don't give all Christ has for me
Just the shadow is enough

Give me the things which will tickle my ears
Only things which are positive you see
Anything else will bring discomfort to me
Just don't speak them, so I'll feel good

The shadows a reflection of the cross
Anything that distracts from the Lord
Too often the programs we have in our churches
You don't hear taught the message of the cross

They make all types of nick-nack's
Playing all types of games
But bless God don't expect me
To have a message about the Lord

That's why our churches are lukewarm
They avoid teaching all of God's word
They only speak things which tickle the ears
Of the ones which come to the church

That's why God said, He'll spew them out
He can't count on you to be found faithful
To teach the whole council of God
There's nothing that should be left out

That's why most people in the pews
Only listen to man, instead of the Lord
Don't teach politics, sex, or divorce
For you'll make people feel uncomfortable

Don't teach that you must be born again
And bless God don't give an alter call
People I invite, don't shake their life
For I want them to come back again

So the preachers are listening to people
Rather then, thus saith the Lord
We forget that the church is a hospital
Where people come to be fed

We're to live in the light of the resurrection
The shadow of the cross will never do
That's why Christ died on the old rugged cross
To expose darkness for you and me

The darkness that lies, down deep in your soul
To expose it and bring it to light
Will bring a true peace into your soul
If you surrender it all to the Lord

The government is running our hospitals
They want only a patch on your life
Bless God if we give them what they need
They may not get sick again

But our hospitals are more about money
Than to meet the real need you have
Just give them one of our drugs
Which will cause other problems in your life

But God is so much different
If we surrender our need over to him
He'll wipe the sickness totally away
He doesn't do a half job my friend

The reason so many never get healed
Is we don't want to get serious before God
We ask the Lord to heal our sickness
Yet we don't want to follow His will

When we truly get serious before him
We get His attention then He starts listening
He doesn't like a prayer that's not serious
For you'll never give the praise to Him

We need to remember, Christ is our Savior
A Savior is one which meets your needs
So it's time we become serious
By asking the Lord to lead the way

When we become serious before the Lord
We'll see results in all of our life
Our God wants the best for us
Yet sometimes he allows troubles to come

Those troubles aren't to punish us
Their to help us grow stronger in Him
The quicker you surrender it to the Lord
The quicker that trial will pass

So stop fighting the work of the Lord
And let Christ lead the way
You'll be so glad you yielded to Him
You'll come out stronger on the other side

Written On: 1-14-15

THE PIG PEN

No one wakes up one day
And says I want to live
In a pig pen the rest of my life
For I know it will be so fun

Getting to the pig pen
Takes a process which we go through
God woke me up this morning
Just about three o'clock

The bad or good thing about it
Was I hadn't gone to bed till one o'clock
I'd only been a sleep for an hour
And I now laid there wide awake

It was bad for I only got one hour
Of sleep which came to my eyes
It was good because the Lord above
Gave me a principle, to not forget

He took me to the story in the bible
Which the boy wanted his inheritance
And the father gave it to him
You might say what a terrible dad he was

You see this didn't just happen
That one day he decided to leave
With his inheritance his dad would give him
And he would enjoy it the rest of his life

Let's take a look at how he got there
So we need to look at our life
As how that we are measuring up
You might be surprised at where you are

The bible tells us in Philippians 2: 5
"Let his mind be in you
Which is in Christ Jesus"
Yes we need to follow the things of God

This boy didn't start out that day
Saying I want to go to the pig pen
But it was a process he went through
In which brought him to that place

He held a grudge in his heart
Against his dad or maybe his brother
He probably wanted his own way
And it wasn't given to him

As days and weeks passed along
Things started festering in his life
He more than likely became disobedient
To his father which loved him so

He wouldn't do what his father asked
It lasted way to long
Finally coming to that time in his life
He asked for his inheritance to leave

So the first phase to the pig pen
Is to start separating yourself from God
For you think you know what's best
In your life each day which you live

That's a terrible place to be in
For God knows what you need for your life
He'll lead you and he'll guide you
Through every phase in your life

Always giving what's best for you
Sometimes it doesn't seem right
Yet if you'll follow in Christ's footsteps
You'll receive the best things for your life

But when you neglect reading God's word
It starts you down the wrong path
You'll not receive what God has for you
You'll wonder why everything goes wrong

If you learn to obey his leading
Even if it's not comfortable to you
You'll finally want what God has for you
And you'll see how blessed you are

Always remember the Lord would never
Lead you down the wrong path
He'll help you through each trial
You face each day in your life

Communication is so important to us
Talking to Christ every day
For He will speak into your spirit
As you get intimate with Him

Then the next phase you go through
Which leads you farther from Christ
You'll think you know what's best
So you separate yourself from others

Separating yourself from family and friends
Which could help you along the way
For two heads are better than one
When you face the trials on this earth

When each put their heads together
One may see something the other doesn't see
Then when you put your thoughts together
You'll have a better picture as what to expect

Spending much time with the older
Which may not be around much longer
You can glean from their wisdom
For many a trial they've already been through

So separating yourself from others
Is another pig pen you find yourself in
And everything gets worse from that point
As you climb deeper into the pig pen

Then the final phase in life
Is when you run out of resources of your own
You can no longer glean from others
Or any resources God's given to us

This is a phase you don't want
To find yourself in, in life
For very few will ever find their way
To get out of the final pig pen, they're in

Satan's now rejoicing in where he's lead you
Down the path of sin and shame
Now all you're having is a pity party
You'll no longer feel the presence of God

So you start playing the blame game
You start blaming God, and other men
But the place you now find yourself in
You can blame no one but yourself

If you should find yourself
In this terrible place in life
The only way to have a good life
Is repent of what you placed yourself in

You got yourself in the place your in
By pushing the Savior away
Replacing it with the things of this world
Where Satan deceived you, to go there

The world's ways will lead you to Hell
That's where Satan wants you to go
For he knows there's no hope for himself
He wants to take you to Hell with him

But if God hasn't cut you off
There is still hope for you
But you must turn to the Savior
Repenting of the life you're now in

Asking the Lord to forgive you
Of the place in which you're now in
And turn to follow the Savior
Leaving the old life, you find yourself in

Then start seeking the Lord for direction
He'll lead you back to the fold
But you must be committed to follow Christ
There's no other way to heaven

Then find a Christ honoring church
Which believes in the full council of God
Then find a strong believer
Which will take you under their wings

The pig pen is where Satan wants you
But God has a much better place for you
Won't you surrender all to Jesus
You'll never regret making the right choice

Written On: 8-2-15

A BROKEN JESUS

Most people in the world
Are serving a broken Jesus
That's the mentality of most people
As they live their lives each day

They're not grounded in Jesus
Yes, the Jesus of the Cross
Yet the Jesus of the Bible
Is richer than anyone else

He owns the cattle in every field
The wealth in every mine
People think everything upon this earth
They own it, and not God

God up in heaven, owns everything
Which you have on this earth
It's only loaned to us by the Lord
He can take it back any time

The world doesn't like preachers
For they speak to much about money
Yet God speaks about the subject of money
More than any other subject in the bible

Those of the world think that everything
Which they own on earth is theirs
So that makes what they have in life
All theirs and no one else

What they fail to realize
God can cut it off anytime
If he didn't want you to have it
He'd not given it to you in the first place

Sometimes he allows you to have it
For you fail to honor Him
Then He'll laugh in your face
When it finally comes to a head

God wants us to learn the principle of money
As to why and how you get it
When we learn that God is the lender
He gives it to us to bless Him

Its then our eyes will be opened
Will then see what money is for
Without learning the principle of money
Our life can't be fully blessed

But once you get it down deep inside
Your heart as why God gives it to you
You have no choice but to give
Ten percent which is required by God

Jesus taught us the will of the father
While living His life on earth
He wants us to be fully blessed
We show Him, by giving what's required

The tithe is our thermometer
Which shows the Lord we trust Him
When were obedient in paying the tithe
It shows God, we fully trust in Him

When we learn to be obedient
Will start seeing the blessings flow
It's when we get excited about giving
It starts flowing through every phase of our life

If you don't let Satan
Discourage you along the way
You'll then start giving offerings
It's then God starts getting excited with you

God then steps into his abundance of blessings
Pouring his blessing into your life
Don't ask me how that he does it
But He's God, and he pours out on you

Mankind thinks in another way
The more I keep I'll accumulate more
My coffers will keep piling up
For I've learned the principle of saving

Yet God in his infinite mercy
Says give, and it will be given to you
He's saying you're holding onto the money too long
Give and I'll show you what I can do for you

I'll meet every need you have
The more you give I'll bless you so much more
Not just in giving your money
But your life will be totally blessed

It could be when you hold back your giving
Your health will fall totally apart
Or your table will be empty of food
And your pantry will have nothing in it

Your car may always be breaking down
Your house always needing repairs
You're constantly taking someone to the doctor
All because you fail to pay your tithes

Your tithe tells the Lord that you trust him
With your life being placed in his hands
Yet Satan will plant a seed in your heart
If you don't pay them, you'll still be blessed

Don't listen to the voice of the deceiver
He'll destroy your life anyway he can
He'll tell you that paying tithes isn't important
To get along in this life on earth

Yet God is speaking to everyone
If you don't pay your tithes as a Christian
You are showing to me you don't love me
From deep down inside your heart

By not loving me, from down deep in your heart
You'll start living your life for yourself
That's where Satan wants you to live
For you'll start wavering from the Cross

The longer you trust Satan's ways
Rather than trust the bible written for you
You could end up in the place, where He'll cut you off
For you wavered to far from the cross

You may say, "What do you mean by that"
The world's ways take priority in your life
They start drowning the Savior out
To the place you know longer hear Him

The things of this world take priority
You'll know longer have time for God
For sports, vacations, and things of this life
Are first in all that you do

At some point the world cries out louder
That's when the Lord will have to cut you off
For you now have become dead on the vine
The vine being the Lord Jesus Christ

Then once you have been severed
From the vine, the Lord Jesus Christ
You can't never be placed back on the vine
Dead vines can't be revived

If you should find yourself wavering
Please don't wait another moment
Christ wants you to repent of your sins
He'll forgive you, and renew you again

But if you keep putting it off
No one can be guaranteed another day
Won't you get your life in order today?
By surrendering everything to the Lord?

Then follow the road map, the Bible
Read it each and everyday
Asking the Holy Spirit to reveal to you
What you need for that very day

Then apply that truth to your life
Without applying it, you'll fail the Lord
Disobedience will send you down the wrong road
And it will send you straight to hell

Won't you get your house in order?
Time is running out my friend
The Lord could return any day
And your life could be snatched from you

We have no guarantee for tomorrow
Yet right now you have a choice to make
Will it be, "Yes Lord, I will follow you?"
Or will you put it off for eternity

When you put things off it makes it easy
To put it off, never to think about it again
God's word says he'll not always strive with man
Don't let Christ separate himself from you

Surrender to Christ this very day
Ask him to forgive you of your sins
Then turn from the ways of your past
That's the most important step you'll make

If you mean it with all your heart
Jesus will accept you into his fold
Then from that time forward
Christ will walk with you everyday

Should you ever find yourself wavering
Quickly repent and follow the Lord
So your life will be prepared for heaven
Every moment you live on this earth

You don't want to be one left behind
For Hell won't be a beautiful place
But Heaven is where you'll want to be
In the presence of our Savior and Lord

No, Jesus is not broken
As so many believe on this earth
They say he's not relative for us today
So we'll only trust ourselves

Yet God's word never changes
As those of the world change everyday
You'll always know what God requires of you
Yet with the world they keep moving the goal

You must decide who you will follow
The one which has given us all that we need
Or one which always keeps you confused
I'll follow Jesus, He's the only way

Written On: 6-24-15

ARE YOU LIVING IN A JAIL?

Most people are living in a jail
Not realizing they're even there
Yet they're not living in the right place
Yet they're satisfied with the life their living

They could have a much greater life
If they would turn from where they are
But they live in a comfort zone
So they lay back and just relax

They say they're afraid to make a step forward
I'm comfortable right where I am
Satan has put fear in their heart
For Satan wants you to stay, right where you are

He knows if you step out of the box
Where he's had you for so many years
You might like the person you'll become
And you'll love serving the Lord

So he feeds you some type of teaser
Which causes you to want to stay there
For he knows the more he teases you
The less chance you'll turn to the Lord

He'll roar every time you try to move
From the comfort zone you're now in
So you let fear control your life
And you continue to live in jail

The Lord has a plan for your life
Too often we fail to spring forth
Yet God is calling out to each of us
Don't hold back, I know what's best for your life

We seem to love that first gear
We've been in it far to long
God wants you to get to the fifth gear
The potential God has for your life

Each gear is not the same for everyone
It's up to us to find, where God would have us
God's saying, "Stop following other people
Seek Me to find out where I need you"

The Lord will show you, when you get serious
In what He would have you to do
Stay at His pace, so you don't get in trouble
Your pace will put you on the wrong road

When we try living our own will
That's when we put ourselves in jail
Many times we'll never come out of it
For we have stayed there, too long

Many people in the jail they're in
Have learned to be comfortable where they are
They don't like the stretching process
Once they leave the comfort zone

It's like those which exercise the body
They'll always stay just where they are
For if there's no pain, there's no gain
To advance from the place their now in

Yet if you will step out of the comfort zone
Asking the Lord to lead the way
Not only will you advance, with Christ in your life
You'll help others along the way

Being in jail is not a picnic
For you're not in the will of the Lord
So Satan desires that you stay there
So you'll not learn to trust the Lord

Failing to trust the Lord instead of yourself
Gives a place in your life for Satan to settle
And if you stays there to long
He'll finally start controlling your life

If you find yourself in this place
There's still hope for you dear friend
As long as you feel God tugging at your heart
The blood will still wipe your sins away

That's why Christ went to the Cross
So you and I could be set free
But we must be willing to step out
And ask Christ to set us free

Not all things lead us to hell
But neglecting to follow God's will for our life
Filling yourself with things of this world
That consumes our time, with no time for Christ

Won't you step out of the jail that you're in
Ask the Lord to cleanse you through and through
So you can be on your way to Heaven
Yes be assured, that you don't end up in Hell

If you are serious in your walk with the Lord
Won't you surrender to Christ right now?
Don't let Satan have another moment
He's already been allowed to live in your life to long

The Holy Spirit will lead you each step you take
There's nothing to be afraid of at all
You'll wonder why you hadn't given Christ
Your total heart many years ago

No you won't be exempt from troubles
Yet the Holy Spirit will guide you through them
Before Christ, you went through them all alone
Now you have the Holy Spirit to guide you along

So please don't wait another moment
Tomorrow may be one day to late
If you surrender all to Him right now
You can be assured of a place in heaven

Written On: 10-3-14

GOOD MORNING

A mom or dad comes in your room
And says, "Good morning son or daughter
It's time to get up
So you'll have time for breakfast"

Mom or dad says good morning to you
For they want your day
To start out on a positive note
So your day will run more smoothly

You walk into the classroom
And your teacher starts the day
By saying good morning to the class
She wanted to get off on the right foot

Those in the work force
Get to work and the boss says
Good morning to everyone
Which arrives to work that day

There's something about saying good morning
Which makes a person feel so good
All because those words good morning
Come from deep down in your heart

There's something about saying good morning
When they're said, with a smile on your face
That changes the total atmosphere
Of the place which you're now at

Have you ever been in a meeting?
Early in the morning and
They got right into the meeting
Without saying good morning

STOP TRYING TO PROVE YOU'RE RIGHT AND START PROVING GOD IS RIGHT

Most times you will find
The meeting is oh so drab
You're not ready to hear negative things
Which gets you off on the wrong foot

Then as you go throughout the day
It seems everything goes wrong
All because your boss
Didn't start out by saying good morning

Well wouldn't it be a better day
If we would say good morning to God
And then spend some time talking to him
On your knees in prayer

Setting a wonderful atmosphere
Knowing you talked to the Lord
The one that's head of everything
And his communication line is always open

So let's talk to the heavenly Father
Setting the pace for the day
Then we will always see
That our day runs so much smoother

Written On: 12-2-11

GOD IS BIGGER THAN OUR MESS

What type of mess are you in?
Do pressures keep pouring in?
It seems that there is no hope
And you think you can't cope with it

Most of the messes we find ourselves in
We have brought upon ourselves
For we're not totally connected
To the Lord Jesus Christ

We tend to step out on our own
On a limb all by our self
We think we can do it on our own
So we let Jesus out of our life

We so often fail to realize
One cord is so easily broken
If we would only ask others
The path would be so much lighter

So as you live your life each day
You fail to believe God's word
Then you wonder why your life
Is filled with so many problems

You live each day for yourself
For you think know one loves you
The reason you feel so bad inside
You're having a pity party all alone

You live day, after day
You become bitter down deep inside
As each day passes along
You blame everyone else for the state you're in

But God gave unto each of us a will
Only we can make things change
The choice God has given to us
To change direction for our life

The first thing you need to do
Is repent of the past life which you've lived
Asking Christ to come into your heart
For your tired of the past life you've lived

The first thing you may think is
It's impossible to change the mess I'm in
But you don't know the God I serve
He is the ruler of this universe

God has always been
And his life will never end
He knows everything you do
You can't hide anything from him

Those things you do behind closed doors
And those things you speak on your phone
You think no one will know about it
Yet God's registering it in his book

He's always looking down on us
He wants us to do the right things
Listening is an important task
Will you listen, or turn him away

You finally asked Christ to come in
To your heart and life that day
The mess in which you got yourself in
Christ wiped ALL your sins away

Yes you sometimes face consequences
Yet Christ goes with you through them
The Lord knows what's best for you
Whether it wipes the consequences away or not

Sometimes God allows you to go through it
Because he knows you can be used for Christ
To reach many more souls for him
It could be you spent time in jail

You see our purpose here upon this earth
Is to lift the banner of Christ high
So use whatever state you find yourself in
Keep praising the Lord as you live for him

Some he may see that you
Get a release from the sin you committed
For he knows you can be a blessing
In the church in which you go

He knows you will not hold back
For you don't do things behind closed doors
That you want others to realize
You live your total life for Christ

If your life is filled with things
Which are totally against the Lord
Depending on the people you're around
You change according to who you face

Yes you may hide things from people
But you can never hide it from God
Remember the Lord sees everything
And the things you do are written in His book

So you must make up your mind
Will I live for Christ each day?
Or will I live my life to please man
And end up in the pit of Hell

For God will not except someone
That tries to live two lives on earth
So my friend who are you living for
Christ wants you to be in Heaven

Know mess in which you're in today
Is too great for God to change
But God wants total commitment
Then your life will totally change

Written On: 3-1-14

WHAT DO YOU DO WITH THE SCRIPTURE

This is something we must get serious about
So many keep it lying on the shelf
They'll never know what's required of them
I'm speaking to people which call themselves Christian

How does the Bible portray a Christian?
It tells us we are a true follower of Christ
This world is full of Christians
Which has no hope for their lives

They walk around with the world on their shoulders
Their so unhappy they look like a prune
Because the Bible is kept on the shelf
Not knowing what serving Christ is about

What do you do with the Scriptures?
That are written for all to behold?
By reading God's Holy Word
We can find out what's required of us

You may say that's not important
For I have ministers which have told it to me
But that's why so many are going to Hell
For many ministers are teaching untruths

There is no minister which is perfect
Every one of them makes mistakes
They're no different than us in the pew
Other than their following the calling God gave them

That's why God's Word makes it very clear
We're to fully study God's Holy Word
To prove ourselves to be approved unto God
So that we're not lead down the wrong road

Why do you think there are so many denominations?
And independent churches around the world
It's because each want to leave certain things out
Which they don't want to believe in God's Word

Am I saying that you shouldn't go?
To any of these churches my friend
You bet I'm not saying that, yet
We need to work together to understand the word

You might see something the other doesn't
So by you digging deeper in God's Word
You may then become much wiser
To help many others along the way

The Bible was written for all to behold
It's not a book so we brag on what we learn
But a special book sent to everyone
So we can brag upon the Lord

Bragging in a sense that we praise Him
And love Jesus with our whole heart
So He will know that we love Him
As we make Jesus number one in our life

Yes without loving the Savior
We'll never make it to heaven above
The only place left for us my friend
Is to be sent to the pit of Hell

My life has been changed overwhelmingly
In the last six or seven years
For I have grown closer to the Savior's side
As I desire his will and not mine

God taught me a principle I don't want to forget
Won't you allow me to share it with you?
If you put it in action, in your life
Your life will also be totally blessed

He'll give you a love for His Holy Word
Which you have never had before
He'll open your eyes to what you've never seen
You'll rejoice in the things he teaches you

You may say hurry up and tell me
I just can't wait any longer to hear
Well the truth is a very simple thing
And you must trust Jesus to lead the way

Here is the truth that God taught me
Stop trying to prove that you're right
For when you study God's word this way
You'll only look for things which prove your desire

Now the other part of the truth God taught me
Is to prove that God's word is right
When you put these phases together
You'll look at the Bible in a different light

Let me give you a perfect example
Which if you get serious before the Lord
You'll see how important this truth is
For you to understand God's Holy Word

Let's take the subject Once Saved Always Saved
This is so controversial among people
Each can prove their point by God's word
And each then believes that it is truth

Each can give you passages
To prove their point to the hearer
Let me ask you a question
Do you believe God's Word doesn't lie?

If you say that God's word doesn't lie
And believe what's written in His word
If we pick one side or the other
We are making God, a liar

If we don't believe God's word as truth
We're taking our side rather than His word
So we end up with a half truth
Instead of the whole truth of God's word

Now let's take a closer look at it
Is either side really lying?
The only answer to it is no
But each are only telling a half truth

Why are they believing a half truth?
Because their only proving they are right
So they're only giving one side of the truth
Leading people down the wrong path

Yes each are telling a truth
But God wants us to have the whole truth
An example the Lord gave to me
Was a tractor trailer on the west coast

He was to bring a load to the east coast
The seal on the load was not to be broken
Until it reached its destination
If broken there would be consequences

Half way to the east coast
He found a secluded place
He broke the seal because he was curious
To what type of load he was hauling

Then he thought he could cover it up
By taking glue, and gluing it together
But when they got to the east coast
They detected it was tampered with

That's the same way with our salvation
God seals us till the day of redemption
God will never break our seal
Yet we as an individual can break it

The reason is that God gave us all a will
He'll never force us to follow Him
So we can say the seal can be broken
By no other one, but ourselves

Then the passage which tells us
No man can snatch us out of God's arms
That passage is one hundred percent right
Yet we ourselves can leave the Lord

Do we one day except Christ into our life
Then a day or two latter leaves His arms?
No it doesn't happen that quickly
Satan deceives us one step at a time

When we yield to Satan's first trick
And don't repent of it each day
They start building up in your lives
Till one day Satan has our soul

The ten virgins God speaks about
Every one of them were believers
But five were wise and five were foolish
Only five of them entered Heaven

What made the difference in the wise virgin's lives
They weren't always trying to live close to the edge
But they were constantly seeking more of God
They seemed to never get enough

But the other five virgins
Were only trying to get by
So when the Lord of the harvest came
They didn't have enough to carry them through

The fire in their lives had gone out
So they had to go out and seek for more
But the Lord of the harvest came
He'd already come before they got back

That's why serving God is a daily walk
There's no time to keep putting things off
We need to serve Christ with our whole heart
That's why He warns us to always be ready

Then the scripture is full of "ifs"
Meaning if you don't follow through with his teaching
That you won't receive His promises
Which He's promised to all believers

Always remember God's word is written to believers
It's then up to us to take it to the lost
So God's word is in the believers hands
What are you going to do with it?

Are you going to hold it for yourself?
Or be obedient to the Lord?
Sharing the good news wherever you go
Loving others into the kingdom

That's why the Lord tells us
To share the good news wherever we go
It will not only help others
It will truly build up your faith

Answers from God, will come to you
When you stop trying to prove your right
And turn it completely around
Proving that God's Word is truth

With the Once Saved Always Saved question
Both are partly right
So now for each of us my friend
How do we pull them together?

Study God's word from both sides
Then get serious before the Lord
Saying, "Lord I don't understand it
For both sides can prove their points"

So Lord I surrender the answer to you
I know your word doesn't lie
After praying one night for some time
God said, read those passages one more time

God, seeing that my heart was now prepared
To receive whatever way He answered
He spoke to my heart so calmly
No man can pluck you out, but you can

The question was now clearly answered
I now have a clear peace in my soul
I've now been changed by God many times
For I thought I had, had the right answers

So we may have to change our thinking
Even when we think we have it all together
Stop being arrogant in your answers
Take time and hear others out

Too often were so quick to blurt out
When God's word tells us so clearly
Be still and know that I am God
Meaning God speaks to us in many ways

Sometimes He speaks through other people
Sometimes He speaks to our mind
Sometimes through the Holy Spirit
But we must take time to listen

We can't be a know it all
For the Lord can't get through to you
For you have blocked the connection
Between you and the Lord

The question asked of each of us
What do you do with the scripture?
For so many, we build on what I want
For we're only trying to prove our point

Won't you stop and give the Lord control
Of your life in all that you do
Even stop following the laws of the land
If they don't measure up to God's plan

God told us to work till He comes
Or if we should leave this world through death
Why would He make such a statement?
If when you're saved, your always saved

The reason he has made that statement
It is possible to lose your salvation
And he wants us to keep focused
On the goal for our life, being Heaven

Heaven will not be for unbelievers
Those which are just playing around
Thinking they can do what they want
And they'll still make it to heaven

Many think they can follow any god
Or they can interpret God's word as they want
We must interpret scripture with scripture
For God's word just doesn't lie

If we find a passage which seems to lie
Be assured your missing something
God doesn't always show us everything plainly
He wants us to spend much time in his word

Very little time can be disastrous
For they're only searching for what they want
In order to feel real comfortable
So they can justify everything they do wrong

But for the true child of God
We can be assured of that place called Heaven
By daily keeping our eyes focused on the goal
Desiring to follow in Christ's steps each day

When we stop trying to prove we're right
And everyone else is wrong
And start proving God's word is true
We'll understand what serving Christ is about

So for you which are not following Jesus
With your whole heart and your soul
Take time right now to surrender to Jesus
All your past life, and begin life a new

You'll never regret making the move
Serving the Lord with your whole heart
The Holy Spirit will lead and guide you
From going down the wrong path

So when you feel his tugging
Don't push the tugging aside
For if you yield to his tugging
It will be the greatest move you ever made

Written On: 9-2 15

WE TALK TO MUCH ABOUT HELL

This phrase is talked about to much
That's what those of the world will say
Yes Hell is a terrible place
For any man, woman, and child to go

The reason so many don't want to hear
Anyone to talk about Hell
It makes them feel very nervous
If they don't have Jesus in their heart

They want to live their lives, as they desire
Speaking of Hell brings conviction to their soul
Making them very uncomfortable, when we talk about
The place they can't find, peace or rest

Not realizing that to know about that place
Yes that place where God has prepared
For Satan and one third of the angels
Which defied God up in Heaven

God did not build it for man on earth
But when Adam and Eve sinned in the garden
Punishment must now come to anyone
Which doesn't have Jesus in their heart

Yes to often Christians are guilty
Of speaking in an arrogant way
Which those of the world put up a guard
Between you and them

As Christians, when we speak about it
Or anything we speak from the Bible
We need to speak it from a heart of love
Always remembering God is love

It's time that every Christian
Learns we're not to beat people over their head
With the way we believe in our heart
We say it is totally God's Word

Many times we make mistakes
Especially when we get all excited
We need to weigh the words we speak
Before they come from our lips
There's a reason the word Hell
Should be spoken wherever we go
God has given us many tools
In His tool box, God's Holy Word

The Christian tool box of God's Word
Is full of tools in His book
God wants us to use then all
Not to toss any from His Word

What are the tools in the Bible?
We're to use from God's Holy Book
They are tools which will get you to heaven
If we use them properly as God intended

Like the tool of what, we've talked about
That terrible place called Hell
The God of Heaven doesn't want you
To end up in the pit of Hell

Speaking of Hell is to awaken us
That we don't end up in that terrible place
It's to make the point that Hell is real
And God doesn't want us to go there

It's to show us the importance of Heaven
It's a place all should desire
For us to be in Heaven
Knowing Jesus will also be there

Yes it's important to talk about Heaven
For God's word speaks much about it
It's a tool to not go to Hell
God doesn't want anyone to fail

Yet the choice is up to each of us
Are we preparing our life to not go there?
If you're not preparing to go there
Be assured Hell is awaiting you

Written On: 6-16-15

THE CLOCK IS TICKING

The clock is slowly ticking
You can't take back the minutes of the past
What you do with the minutes right now
Determines who you'll serve in the here after

God up in heaven is keeping records
What is He writing in his book?
Are the things you're doing this very day
Things that are pleasing or not of the Lord

Are you seeking the Lord with your whole heart?
Loving each moment you spend with Him
The time you spend upon this earth
Brings glory and honor to Christ?

Or is your life filled with so much stuff
It's blocking Christ out of your life
Where the Holy Spirit can't speak to your heart
You feel you have much better things to do

If you find yourself in this situation
And God is speaking or probing your heart
This very moment my dear friend
Please don't push the Holy Spirit from you

Who knows this could be His final call
At the door of your heart today
God said He would not always strive with man
No, we can't just come when we want

As He probes at your heart this very moment
Won't you obediently answer his call?
This could be the last chance you'll have
Before you enter into eternity

If this should be your last day
Or the last time He knocks at your heart
What you decide this very moment
Will determine where you'll spend eternity

All it takes is a total surrender
To our Savior, our Lord, and our King
He's reaching out to you right now
Please don't turn aside from Him

Christ wants you more than you'll ever know
He doesn't want you to end up in Hell
Won't you make this your happiest day
Where heaven will be your final resting place

Don't come to him with just formality
Lay your whole life totally before him
Asking Christ to renew all within you
Promising to leave this old world behind

If you truly mean it with your whole heart
And start serving the Lord every day
Be assured Christ will be awaiting you
When you take your last breath on earth

Written On: 11-7-15

AN ALTAR

How many have heard of an altar?
In most churches across the land
The alter has been removed
For they say it's not important today

Why have they removed the alters
When the alter has been used
Ever since the beginning of time?
Now you say it's no longer important

So many of the altars in our churches
Have been removed from the front of them
Because the Holy Spirit is no longer welcome
He has been replaced with all of those programs

What they fail to realize is
Without the Holy Spirit welcomed there
Their life will never feel conviction
Yes the people which attend the church

That's what Satan's been working towards
For years deceiving man and woman
He knows when the Holy Spirit's removed
The church now is only lukewarm

They'll only go through a formality
Where the Lord will no longer dwell
Then they'll have the heart of so many people
And they'll end up in the pit of Hell

That's why Satan has convinced so many people
The alter is no longer important to man
You're just a fool to spend all your time
It's just like speaking to the wall

But God of Heaven is crying out
Satan is a deceiver and a liar
Hell is assuredly awaiting them
When their present life on earth is complete

He wants to drag all he can with him
Straight to the pit of Hell
Saying, if he must go to the pit of Hell
I'll drag as many as I can with me

You see, Satan doesn't like the altar
He knows that people's needs are met there
That's where their mind gets focused
On the Lord Jesus Christ

We think of altars in our churches
Yet they're not the only place you find them
You can make an altar wherever you go
Just seek the Lord, for the glory to come down

When we seek the Lord with our whole heart
Be assured the Holy Spirit will arrive
So that's where the needs of your life will be met
Dwelling in the presents of the Lord

It's when we get serious before the Lord
We can certainly see people come to Christ
Then we will see miracles taking place
For that's where the Lord truly dwells

Diseases will disappear from people
Tumors will drop off
Doctors don't have the final say
They say there is no hope for you

That's when the Lord loves to begin
When we get serious before him
He knows when he is welcomed
That's when doubts and fear disappear

It's when those doubts and fears disappear
The Lord now has a place to work
When people receive their healing
The Lord is now the one which receives the praise

Its then that man can't take the praise for
What has taken place right before their very eyes
For man has now given up
There's nothing more he can do

It's when we get serious before the Lord
That's when the Lord arrives
And he can now show that he is God
Man can only say it's the Lord

That's our purpose here on this earth
To give praise and honor to Christ
That's why Christ waits so long at times
Because man wants to take the praise

If we would only get before an altar of God
At church or in a closet of prayer
Closing out the cares of this life
Asking the Lord to take over our life

It's when we get serious before the Lord
Realizing the Lord is our only hope
Not just to meet a need in our life
But wanting salvation to come to our soul

That's when the Lord will arrive in your presence
He knows all glory will be given to Him
For you have now set aside all your thinking
Turning your total life over to Christ

Your life is now ready for Christ to arrive
The needs of your life now can be met
Making the Lord so very happy
He can now change your whole life

Your past life will no longer excite you
Satan will no longer be number one in you
You've now made Christ number one in all you do
That's when He will totally revamp your life

Yes you'll never want to turn back
To the old life you once lived
For now you want to praise the Lord
Letting Christ shine, through every phase of your life

How can you know who has your life?
Take a look at the life your living
Who or what, do you spend most of your time with?
That is the God which your now serving

So how are you living your life today?
Does Satan have control of you?
If he does be assured Hell is awaiting you
Where you'll be tormented for eternity

Never to find peace and rest
You'll be tormented for all eternity
Not only to be tormented by fire
You'll remember all the times you rejected Christ

Yes, you'll remember the word of God
You'll remember what Christ did for you
That He died, was buried, and rose again
So every man, woman, and child, could be set free

Yes, Hell will be an unhappy place
You'll never have another chance
To surrender all to Jesus
The life you now live determines your final destination

So, won't you make an altar before the Lord
Surrendering your whole heart and life to Christ
So at the end of your life on this earth
God won't have to say, "Depart from me"

So live your life for Christ right now
And daily keep your life cleansed
By daily spending your time in God's presence
Enjoying your life walking with Christ

Then when you stumble along the way
You quickly repent of that sin
So God's book is wiped clear of your sins
Then God can say, my child enter in

Written On: 11-7-15

YOUR BODY IS THE TEMPLE OF GOD

Your body is the temple of God
He said it in His Holy Word
So each one of us must use it
To bring glory to the Father above

To many are using their body
For only what they desire
When God says it's the temple of God
He speaks of purity and nothing else

We must measure up to the Bible
Which is our rule book on this earth
If we don't desire to follow his leading
God designed Hell for Satan and his followers

When we think of what the bible stands for
Purity to shine for all to see
Not purity as man has designed it
But purity to please the Lord

Man is defiling the body
In so many ways on this earth
Sex is the greatest defilement to man
For it is seen everywhere you go

God designed sex in the bond of marriage
Yes it is a beautiful design
For those which use it in the proper way
God's blessing is upon it

How do we defile this body with sex?
Let's take a look at some of the ways
Experiencing sex before marriage
Is forbidden by God's Holy Word

Why has God designed it that way?
God knew it would cause many problems later
Some have had sex with many partners
With diseases being passed on to others

Then many will get pregnant
Not even caring for the one they had sex with
They only want to fulfill their own desires
Then they'll move on to another person

But because of that one time having sex
You end up getting the girl pregnant
Now your problems start multiplying
All because of not keeping your body pure

Some will then get married
When they had no desire for it in the first place
Now you run out on the one you married
For you weren't ready to be tied down

Then others will get an abortion
Thinking it will solve their problem
The girl has multiple problems later
Both mentally and also guilt

So often it carries into your marriage
You can't enjoy the sex God designed
For those which had sex before marriage
Satan keeps bringing it up in your life

If you are one that has caught this disease
You need to quickly repent
And save your sex until marriage
God designed it for husband and wife

Some use sex in other ways
With one of the same sex
God declares that it's an abomination
And it will sent you straight to Hell

Sex is designed for only marriage
For only those of the opposite sex
Then we're to serve the Lord to the fullest
Wanting to please the Lord in all that we do

Once you become of age to get married
If you feel temptations coming to you
Ask the Lord to send unto you one to marry
And control yourself until He does

Then once you have found that girl
Set the date for you to get married
For it's God's will that you should marry
Than to have sex and burn in Hell

There are other ways to defile this body
Which God has shown to us
We can defile it with alcohol and cigarettes
Also by eating too much food

We can defile our body
By placing things in it we shouldn't
Like listening to filthy music
Or watching filthy things on TV

We can pick up books which will defile us
Supporting pornography of men and women
And defile our minds with witchcraft
Which cause us to have problems in life

The bible says what we defile our minds with
Is what we will become
So we need to stay away from those things
Leaving the Lord to direct our life

How can we take care of this temple of God?
By feeding wholesome things in it
You might say what are wholesome things?
Let's take a look at some of them

Number one thing each of us must do
Surrender our whole life over to Christ
Turning from the past life we've lived
Desiring all that Christ has for us

Spending much time in the Bible
Allowing the Holy Spirit to lead the way
Asking Christ to feed your mind
With thing which will help you grow in Christ

Oh you can read other wholesome books
Which have great morals
But never put them first
Before God's Holy Word

God's word declares that we fail
For lack of knowledge in our life
We fail to lift up the Lord Jesus Christ
We fail to search for helps to help us

We've become satisfied just where we are
And, bless God, don't rock the boat
I'm comfortable just where I am
Searching will make me uncomfortable

Yet what we fail to realize
It's the Holy Spirit probing our heart
Which keeps us on the right path
Which will keep us out of Hell

God has written in His word
We're to study to show ourselves approved unto God
A workman that needeth not to be ashamed
Rightly dividing the word of truth

The Bible has the answer
To every problem we face in life
That's why serving Jesus
Is the best move you'll ever make!

The Bible is the living word
God gives, as we can handle it
It's the Holy Spirit that will revel to you
When it's time to take the next step

Never try getting ahead of God
Allow the Holy Spirit to lead the way
Be assured when you allow Him to lead you
You'll enjoy each step, he leads you to take

If you place unwholesome things in your mind
Which Satan would have you to do!
You will be on the wrong road
The road which leads straight to Hell

The bible teaches what we put in our bodies
Is what we will become!
Won't you fill your mind with wholesome things
So your destination will be heaven?

Written On: 10-23-15

WORK OUT

When people tell you they worked out
We think of those going to a gym
With all these different kinds of machines
Which work all of your muscles

The Bible, when talking about work out,
Has a much different take on it
It says we're to work out our salvation
With fear and with trembling

That means we're not to pick and choose
The things we want to believe in God's word
We're to take the word seriously
By putting the word of God into practice

Morals seem to be the first thing
That are not preached from our pulpits
We don't want people to take offense
We just want all to feel good

The problem with us not preaching it
When the Bible tells us to preach God's word
If we hold back what God requires of us
We will send many people to Hell

These things were taught many years ago
Yet were not taught out of a heart of love
We drove more people from the Lord
Rather than lead them to the foot of the Cross

If God teaches it in His Word
We need to teach it from the pulpit
Out of a total heart of love
In order to give people the whole truth

Many preachers say they teach the whole truth
Yet they leave so much untouched
All they're teaching people in the pew
It's alright to teach a social gospel

Why is it we should not smoke
Or love drinking from the bottle
Or put drugs in our bodies when
You can't find them mentioned in the Bible?

Yet there is a specific reason to not
Partake of any of these things
Yes God's Word makes it very plain
Yet few teach the reason why

The main reason we should not partake of them
God says were to keep our bodies pure
Yes our bodies are the temple of God
And outsiders are watching us

When others of the world watch us,
Who smoke and go to church,
You're sending a mixed signal
That it's alright to do as the world does

Then what you are doing
Is planting thoughts in their minds
They're no different than those outside
So why should I waste my time?

But when we point out the reasons why
We as a believer should not partake of it
Yes believers shouldn't partake of it
For it will drive people farther from Christ

Explain that so many have lung cancer
Many diseases they cause in the body
Caused by the cigarettes you say you enjoy
Yet it's not pleasant, who you've become

That's a trick that Satan uses
The advertisements show beautiful girls
That makes it oh so pleasant
That everyone else is doing it

And the bottle which so many love
Most will say it's only a social drink
Yet no one can guarantee you
That you won't become an alcoholic

Once you've gotten hooked on the bottle
You socialize more and more
One day you become an alcoholic
Then you can't kick the habit

Then you end up with cirrhosis of the liver
Then your life comes to an end
All because Satan used other people
To convince you social drinking was alright

How about all those people you hang around
They are all smoking that weed
They shame you into taking a puff
Which makes you feel so good

Finally you become hooked on them
Then someone slips you a pill
It doesn't cost you anything
Yes that first pill they gave you

But once you came down from that high
Your body demands more
But now you have to pay for
The next pill, that will make you feel good

You finally have to go out and steal
In order to get money for your habit
Eventually you lose your job
Which provides the needs of your family

Then there are those which take a peek
At a web site which popped up on your computer
Instead of clearing it from your eyes
You go deeper into pornography

You think you can handle it
But God warns us to keep our lives pure
By peeping at that pornography
Your mind can't handle it any more

So you keep going deeper in sin
The Bible teaches us to not lust
Lust will take you on the wrong road
It can even cause you to kill

They say most all people that have murdered
Started out on pornography
So if they can't get what they want
They'll kill with no remorse about it

Lust is such a powerful thing
Not just for sex you demand
But lust for anything that belongs
To another person no matter who they are

The Bible teaches we're to be content
With the things he provides for us
For when we lust for what others have
We will never have a peace in our heart

The sad thing is that these things
Are common in the churches on earth
So we are sending people to Hell
When the church should be a haven of rest

It's time to get back to the basics
Teaching the whole truth not leaving things out
And be sure, we teach them in context
Rather than make the Word, a pleaser of man

That's why there are so many denominations
They picked and choose what they want to believe
And bless God no one should question
Even if you prove I'm wrong, I'll not change

So many of the things we teach in our churches
Are nothing more, than a half-truth
For half-truths make people feel good
And we can fill our churches with people

Numbers are more important to us
Than to be sure it's the word of God
God teaches us if we don't follow his word
He will eventually spew us out

Yes a Christian who has accepted Christ into their heart
And lived for him every day
But got caught up in believing their preacher
Without testing his words, with the word of God

If we get caught up in these things
Yes I'm talking about Christ followers
He will eventually cut you off
Never to be reconnected to the Lord again

So don't find yourself drifting
If you do, quickly repent,
So the book, which God's keeping,
Will be empty of all sins

Daily seek the Lord each day
Asking Christ to reveal to you
The truth He wants to teach you
So you'll not fall from the grace of God

Written On: 4-7-14

WHO, WHAT, AND WHY DO YOU GIVE

God wants to teach each of us
He says, what is it you have
He wants all of us to be truthful
For all the things in which we own

Most say they don't have much
But you'd be surprised, just what you're worth
Just grab a paper and pencil
And start writing down everything you own

As you write down everything
You'll be amazed as to what you're worth
And the greatest thing, you can't put value on,
Is if you've given your whole life to Christ

Yes all these things mean nothing
Until you've given your life to Christ
For the things you own in your life
Are not blessed by the Lord

But when you surrender all to Him
God's eyes are opened wide
And he starts seeing your heart
That your whole life belongs to Him

Yes it is then God can began to work
In the life in which you live
For he is totally convinced
He now can trust you to honor Him

You see without our total commitment
We tend to tell God what we'll do
But once he has your whole heart
Your life changes to, what I can do for Him

The greatest thermometer of a Christian's life
Is in our method of giving
If we can't be obedient to Christ
We can't be blessed in what we give

For he is not a God
That is up in Heaven, to be manipulated
But the Lord requires obedience
That's when he can work in our lives

Who is it you're giving to/
When we place money in the offering plate
Are you thinking of what it could have been used for?
Or have you released it unto the Lord

God cannot bless anything
If we put stipulations on it
The money in which we give
Is our first fruits, yes our tithes

Now once you learn to give
From a total heart of love
God now has your attention
That your heart is now loving him

Now when you pick up your Bible
And you read it every day
You'll read that if you really want to be blessed
We will then start giving offerings

You quickly pick up the dictionary
It says that it's a contribution
And you now realize that it is
Anything above a tithe

You may say, how is it not your tithe?
Because a tithe is required by God
If we don't pay our tithe
We are a thief and a robber

But an offering starts you on the road
Placing you where Christ can start blessing you
Blessings come from the Lord
All from a total heart of love

That's when God opens the coffers of heaven
He already owns everything
So stop depending on your own mind
In order to figure God's plans out

The problem with trying to figure God out
There's not a soul, which can understand his whole plan
For God's ways aren't our ways
He pulls strings not known to man

The answers can come in many packages
Through people we meet every day
It can come through unknown people
Which we will never know in our life

You say, how can unknown people
Know what your needs in life are
God speaks to the hearts of other people
To do things they have never done before

For those people, which God speaks to,
Already know how God blesses people
If they are obedient to God's voice
Great blessings will start flowing

Yes the Lord wants you to be blessed
But if you hold things for yourself
You'll never know what blessings are
Greed will take you down the wrong road

But if you will listen to God's voice
He'll bless you in ways you can't explain
It could be you gave to missions
You gave all your money from your savings account

God had spoken to your heart
Then you gave out of a heart of love
You were obedient to God's voice
You now had bills you could not pay

On Monday morning the mailman came
He handed you a letter
You looked at it, yes it was plain
With no return address on it

As you opened the envelope
Excitement came to your heart
For the check you found inside of it
Was ten times more than the bill you paid

After you got past the excitement
The Holy Spirit spoke to your heart
To pay that hospital bill of a certain person
You now had a real big choice to make

Will I once again obey the Lord
Or will I keep it for myself
But you began thinking it through
And you were obedient to his voice

Now you proved to the Lord
That whenever you hear his voice
You will listen to what he tells you
Never to put yourself first

Many of the world and those in churches
May say you are foolish, to give away everything
But that tells you whom you're trusting
Their thinking is not of the Lord

Now won't you listen very closely
I don't recommend for anyone
To give away everything
Unless you have heard from the Lord

Too many listen to themselves
They get caught up in their own thinking
Rather than follow the plans of the Lord
So when they get in trouble they blame the Lord

Stop trying to get ahead of God
Start communicating with Christ each day
So there will be no question
When you hear the voice of God

So because you hear the voice of God
And followed as he spoke to you
God took you to higher heights
Than you ever dreamed you could go

Won't you start following God's plan
Rather than follow the voice of the world?
The voice of the world is of Satan
That will lead you straight to Hell

Yet God's ways are real rewarding
They'll prepare you for Heaven
So, won't you follow God's ways
So you won't miss heaven?

Written On: 4-6-14

WHOSOEVER TALKS TO THE MOUNTAIN

There are so many which have
Mountains standing in their way
Some mountains may be very small
Most mountains you don't know you have

For Satan has sent that mountain your way
He has been so sly to send it to you
You are so caught up in those things
You don't realize the mountain is harming you

We're not talking about a mountain
With trees growing all over them
Where birds build nests in there branches
And hoot owls love to hoot

There are so many mountains in your life
Satan doesn't want you to know who you've become
So Satan is so sly how he sends them to you
You don't realize they came from him

Satan is a thief an a robber
He'll slowly take those good things from you
He makes his things so appetizing
You won't realize where he's taking you

You stand in the checkout line
A beautiful girl on the front of a magazine
As you take a closer look at her
She's smoking a cool cigarette

It says if you smoke this cool cigarette
You will feel so cool
You'll fit in with all your friends
Which have already found it cool

What Satan fails to tell you
That at your later years of life
You'll be gasping for your breath
Then you'll start blaming it on the Lord

But God gave each of us a will
He's knocked at your heart many times
But you kept turning the Savior away
You can blame no one but yourself

One of your buddies which you were with
Enticed you to take a puff
From a joint which he handed you
He said it would make you feel good

That joint in which you caved into
Started controlling your life
You started hiding behind closed doors
Showing that you knew it was wrong

Before long someone drops you a pill
Now you are totally depending on it
And it caused you, to do many things
Which are so bad in this life you live

For you are so dependent on it
Every time you come down from the high
You don't have money to buy it
So you'll steal, kill, or destroy to get it

Yet God is still probing your heart
He wants you to turn from your wicked ways
For he has the best plan for your life
He will never lead you astray

There are so many different mountains
Which different people face in life
You don't have to be a worldly person
Yes, it happens to believers in the church

Health problems come to so many of you
Sometimes we do things our own way
Because of not taking care of our bodies
God says we're to take care of them

Sometimes God allows us to go through them
To help us grow in the Lord
If we keep our eyes on Jesus
Be assured your life will come out stronger

Then sometimes we go through problems
Our life will come to an end
It's not because he loves us less
For you truly had let your light shine

Some shine for Jesus all their lives
Many say, why would God allow it to happen?
But because our life now came to an end
Your life then begins to shine much brighter

Always remember, our ways aren't God's ways
And God's ways are not as we see them
Many times we cannot explain it
But be assured the Lord has our best at heart

Other areas in which we face in life
As a believer in Jesus Christ
We tend to want our own will
Rather than follow the will of the Lord

How about you paying your tithes
If you don't, God calls you a thief or robber
Many times God will allow you to fall deep in debt
All because that's the only way to get your attention

You may say, why does the Lord
Allow a Christian's life to be taken away
But it could be their life would be a testimony
Your life for God can shine much brighter

Sometimes we may never know
Why God allows certain things to happen
Until later years of our life
Or once your life has passed on

Be assured the Lord knows the puzzle
And how each piece fits together
So trust the Lord to lead your life
So pieces of the puzzle, will not be missing

For if you do not accept God's will
For the life you live each day
Then God will have to pick someone else
To fit in the puzzle where you are missing

For when the puzzle is completed
The Lord will then return to this earth
To receive all of those with him
That has been fitted into the puzzle

So won't you get on board today?
Don't let the world dictate your life
But surrender all to Jesus
And follow his directions for your life

Then when your life on earth is completed
The Lord will say to you, "Welcome home
For you have been found faithful
To what I have required of you"

Written On: 3-30-14

A PARABLE OF A BLOWER

As a man works in his lawn each week
He takes pride in the work he does
He makes sure it's weed wacked
For he wants the job well done

He buys the best equipment
The equipment you use, makes all the difference
Then it takes something else that's important
That's pride to get the job well done

Too many do a haphazard job
They take no pride in what they do
All their concerned about
Is to get the lawn completed right now

The problem with this mentality
Is it follows you through, all that you do
In and outside your house
And the car in which you drive each week

You might say what does this
Have to do with a blower you have
The blower has a lot to do
With how your yard looks like to others

After you finish mowing
And weed whack the lawn
There is now grass on the walk
And on the driveway to the garage

No matter what type equipment you have
It is never a good job
If you use the best of equipment
Or the cheapest one you can buy

Some may say, what do you mean
That neither one is a good job?
If you don't blow the walks off
As well as the driveway to the garage

Once you blow the sidewalks off
You can see the good job you've done
Then as you look at other lawns
You see the bad jobs they have done

The cheap blower which most people use
Won't do a good job on the walks
For once you finish blowing them off
You'll still see grass on the side walk

But the job done by the best blower
Does a superb job for you
The grass is blown off the walk
People say what a good job it does

People always love a job well done
Even though it may be more expensive
Then others only look at cheap
It reflects the life they live

As we think about this parable
What can we learn from it?
Let's take a closer look
To see how it might speak to our life

Too many people are like a cheap blower
All they do is blow some wind
They tell you all the things they do
Yet they never follow through with them

They tell you they will share the gospel
With everyone they meet each day
That's what many tell you in the church
As they worship each and every week

They blow a little steam each week
Telling everyone all the work they do
In spreading the gospel every week
Yet all they're doing is deceiving others

Their deceiving people everywhere
Telling people they're doing God's work
The things they do for Christ each week
Is nothing more than deceiving man

But using the best of equipment
Is like using all the resources you have
Finding out all you can about Christ
To live out Christ in your life

The force the expensive blower produces
Is like a person who truly loves the Lord
They want all Christ has for them
They'll keep working till they reach their goal

They never follow other people
They daily seek the will of God
Searching the scriptures every day
And praying for God's will for their life

As they seek God's will every day
The Lord gently speaks to their heart
When they hear God speak to them
They quickly follow his direction for them

Not trying to cut corners to reach their goal
Knowing God wants us to follow Him
For he has our best at heart
Heaven will be waiting, when they pass the test

Satan will try tempting you
To vary from the plans of God
Yet you determine to not give in
To any trick Satan sends your way

You not only read God's Holy word
You follow the directions to a tee
And when your life on earth is complete
You'll then be ushered into heaven

Written On:5-11-14

<u>WHO WILL ENTER HEAVEN</u>

Too often as we live our lives
Here upon this earth each day
We want to pick and choose
The people which will go to heaven

Yet we need to be so careful
How we pick and choose people
For the Lord's plans are so much different
Than the plans men has on this earth

Yes there are standards we must live by
The standards are found in God's word
Yet too often we set our own standards
By what we desire for our life

The Word of God is very specific
We must fit it all together
From the book of Genesis
To the last book of Revelation

We can't pick and choose what we desire
Leaving most of the scriptures behind
For the Bible is like a puzzle
It all must be fit together

If you link the wrong pieces in a puzzle
The rest will not fit together
Then the puzzle will not be complete
It will be nothing more than a mess

That's the way with so many Christians
We think we have it all together
And bless God no one can change me
For I can prove it in God's word

So we launch out to find passages
To prove that we are totally right
So we miss the things the Lord
Puts in our life to fit it together

The puzzle ends up with so many red flags
You're questioning who is the god I serve
It all leads to one thing
You try and prove that you are right

Let's go to a passage in the Bible
A parable spoken by Jesus Himself
It's hard for us upon this earth
To comprehend what He is saying

There's the passage of the farmer
Which had a harvest to bring in
So in the morning at six o'clock
He told the first worker how much he would pay

He agreed to work for the wage
And was happy to do the work
Until he found out the farmer had hired others
At different hours throughout the day

He hired some at nine and other at noon
Some at three and others at five o'clock
There was only one hour left
For the one he hired at five

The farmer had a certain amount
Of work to be done that day
Realizing at each point throughout the day
He needed more men to accomplish it

Yet the odd thing about hiring each
They all were paid the very same wage
The first thing that most would say
It wasn't fair for all the others

The Bible says to whom much is given
That to them much is required
So the one hired at the first hour
Much was required of him

This flows through each hired
At different hours of the day
You see God knows what to expect of you
We're not to compare ourselves with others

Well when the end of the day came
And each lined up to be paid
The farmer paid each the same
For the work each had done that day

Most would say that he wasn't fair
And that's so true in the eyes of man
Yet we fail to put the puzzle together
We believe everyone should be treated equally

Yet what we fail to realize
Each agreed to work for what they were offered
Who are we, to complain?
That the master just wasn't fair

You say no one pays a workers
A days wage if he only works an hour
But you fail to realize
The Lord does it all the time

The farmer explained to the people
The ownership belonged to me
And I can do as I like
With what belongs to me

Death bed conversions you say aren't fair
What about the thief on the cross
For Jesus said unto him
This day you shall be with me in paradise

You see God's ways aren't always our ways
The Lord dishes grace out to any man
Which walks with the Savior
Won't you give the Lord your whole heart?

Now what is the picture of each man hired?
We have a specific work to do
Whatever the Lord lays out for you
God always requires the best from you

The mentality of most people
If the one hired last gets paid the some
Then I will just goof off
For I have to be out here all day

You failed to realize you made a commitment
The Lord requires the best you have
That's where the rewards that are given out
If you're faithful you'll receive it

But if you spend your time goofing off
You will not receive a reward
You'll have to hang your head in shame
When you face the Lord on judgment day

The one which has a death bed experience
Doesn't have a reward to place at Jesus feet
He didn't have time to work in God's kingdom
For death arrived too soon to work

It's time we stop comparing ourselves with others
But compare ourselves with God's Holy Word
Then leave the rest for the Holy Spirit
To guide our lives as we work each day

It will keep us on the narrow road
Where few people are walking on
Yes most that say their walking with Christ
Are deceiving themselves because of how they live

The Lord is preparing a place for those
Which are faithful to Christ each day
How, are you measuring up
To God's marvelous Holy Word?

It's time we stop playing around
Working hard for Christ each day
So we will have a crown
To lay at the Savior's feet

Yes the one with the death bed experience
Will make it to heaven my friend
Yet death bed experiences that are made
At that late hour of the day

Eleventh hour grace means if you're able
To read this poem there's still time
To reach out to the Savior
And surrender your total life to Christ

Don't put it off another day
Tomorrow may never come
And you'll be thrown in the pit of Hell
Yes the next moment may be too late

Today is the day of salvation
Christ is waiting for you this very hour
Won't you surrender all to Jesus
While there's still time for you to choose

Written On: 9-11-14

WHO WILL ENTER IN

Our attitude is so very important
Have you checked it out, lately
That's the problem most people have
They never stop to analyze their life

Their life is filled with sin
Right down to the very core
They think they have it all together
Yet their life proves other wise

You wonder why all your friends
Seem to be shunning you
When you go around them
They seem to go another way

Or there always making excuses
Why they can't hang around
It really is a cop out
To get away from your presence

They see the way you act
When you are in their midst
They don't want you to rub off on them
For they don't want to become who you are

You've never believed in the Lord Jesus Christ
So your life is formed after the world
You don't have anything in common
That your friends could feel good about

Yes, you may go to church on Sunday
Sing the songs everyone else sings
Then listen to a special song
Which someone sang that day

You put a dollar in the offering plate
You made sure everyone saw you do it
You thought others wouldn't think you're stingy
For you participated in the giving

Oh yes you pretended that you listened to
The sermon which the preacher preached
Yet your heart was far from the preaching
Thinking of what you'll do, when you got out of church

You were so glad the sermon came to an end
But they had that alter call
It seemed the preacher kept talking to you
But bless God you'd stand your ground

Your friend which was sitting beside you
Hearkened to the salvation call
It made you so mad inside
Your friend would no longer have your interests

The final prayer was now offered
You quickly got up from your seat
The preacher was there to shake your hand
Along with many of the other people

They asked you to come back again
It was so good to have you there
You got more bitter by the minute
So you raced quickly to your car

As you raced out into the highway
You pulled out in front of a car
Your life was snatched from you
Now just what would happen to you?

You face the Savior up above
It became the worse day of your life
For when the Savior spoke to you
He said you can't enter into rest

You will be terribly tormented
There'll never be any end in sight
You had wasted away your days on earth
Rejecting the Savior of your Soul

But let's take a look at your friend
Which responded to the alter call
His life was changed at the alter
For he surrendered all to Christ

He went through many a trial
As he walked upon this earth
Yet every time he faced those trials
He made sure they were covered with the Blood

He finally faced the King of Kings
On that great judgment day
The Savior welcomed him with open arms
Saying he could now enter into his rest

The decision now is in your hands
What will you do with your life today?
The next breath you may take
Could very easily be your last breath

Written On: 4-27-13

AS A MAN THINKETH IN HIS HEART

Man thinks so many things
Many things are good for your life
And many things are bad things
Depending on what's in your heart

What you fill your mind and soul with
Gets embedded down deep in your soul
What is it you're doing?
Make sure you're fed with good things

How much of your time do you watch TV?
Watching programs which tear you down
You constantly hear curing
And you're not bothered with them

In fact they all make you laugh
It's being embedded in your heart
Curing, swearing, and killing
And all of those sexual things

Many think it's not hurting them
Yet it's doing more harm than you think
The Bible warns us so plainly
What we feed our minds with, we become

Who are you putting your trust in
Is your trust totally in the Lord
Or is your mind so cluttered
With all the things of this world

Many minds are so cluttered with sports
The Lord takes second place in their life
You only serve the Savior
If you can fit him into your schedule

When this takes place in your life
You're serving the wrong god
For sports have become your god
There's no place for God to enter in

You know longer can hear God speaking
For sports keep drowning the Savior out
The deeper you get involved
The farther you're driven from the Lord

This world has so many things
That will drown the Savior out
We must always be on guard
To keep from drowning the Savior out

Self must always be set aside
Serving self will lead you on the wrong road
The more you let self-control you
The farther it will lead you from the Lord

If you stay in that mode to long
You will totally lose out with Christ
And the nudging of the Holy Spirit
Will eventually fizzle out

If you own or run a business
Not putting Christ first in your life
The things you think down deep inside
Will overwhelm you as you live your life

The way you treat those you work with
You can be bitter from deep within
And if you treat them harshly
Quality work will not get done

If you treat and lift up people,
Which work under you each day,
Like they are worth someone
You will build confidence in them

They will want to do more for you
Because they feel good inside
And won't want to be a wimp
They know their life will be built up

But if you're always putting people down
It will reflect, who you are
And as it reflects who you are
People will be a reflection of you

What type person do you want to become
The choice is totally up to you
But God wants us to build others up
In order to be a powerful force for him

If you want peace inside of you
You need to put on the Lord Jesus Christ
Jesus will reflect himself through you
Making you a person just like him

Loving Jesus is what it takes
To become a powerful force on this earth
Reflecting Jesus is what it takes
To bring others to the Cross

So if you're living a negative life
Turn one hundred eighty degrees around
And you'll never regret the choice
That your life has now taken on

Written On: 7-1-14

WHERE DO WE STAND TODAY

There are some important things
Which are left out of our lives
We have totally left out Holiness
It has weakened the church today

We get mad when people bring it up
Yes, pastors in churches across the land
We have bought into political correctness
So we have totally weakened our land

The Lord requires us to stand up
And declare the whole counsel of God
It's when we start leaving things out
We start drifting from the presence of God

The word purity is almost never discussed
For we've bought into the ways of this world
The world's ways are run by Satan
Yes their always created by him

He's so slick in all he does each day
Hiding completely behind the scene
Probing the hearts and lives of people
Putting doubts in the minds of Christians

Too often we yield to all his tactics
He takes a small step at a time
He'll never show you where he's taking you
If he did, we wouldn't follow his leading

He tickles your ears a little at a time
Tricking you to believe things are alright
He'll have people to shame you
If you're against the tricks he's set forth

He'll start with those who are leaders
Telling them to convince the people
Then when they get enough on their side
He then moves in for the kill

We blame all these things on the government
Yes they are a part of Satan's plan
But the real blame for all of our problems
We can blame no one but ourselves

If the church would do what they're supposed to do
The world wouldn't be in the mess there in
Yes, we as believers in Jesus Christ
Needs to totally get involved in our government

Quit caving into Satan's tactics
Which he says the church isn't to get involved
But every time we cave into his tactics
The church become so much weaker

The church is so involved in programs
They're not teaching the whole counsel of God
So the church has become so weak
For it is no different than the world

There's nothing in the church to run to
People of the world are all looking for something
So the world is providing a short fix
By telling the church they need more programs

So the church is doing what the world does
Having all types of those programs
And bless God don't preach what's in the bible
Just tell us story's that will make us laugh

And oh yes you can't forget those jokes
They make us so happy you see
But don't have a sermon on do's and don't
They're not appropriate for the church today

And bless God don't you expect us
To come to church more than one time a week
And cut the service off at twelve o'clock
So I don't have to wait in a line at the restaurant

And if you preach those powerful sermons
Which causes conviction to come
I'll start a click against you
And get you voted out of the church

We've wooed the people asleep to long
They think conviction comes from the preacher
But if they only knew the Word of God
They'd know conviction comes from the Lord

People are so blind to the gospel
They can't hear the voice of God anymore
There headed straight to Hell
And they don't even realize it

The preachers have convinced them too long
That they are a child of God
For they are a member of their church
An bless God I don't want to lose them

So they are making people feel good
Deceiving each that they are alright
The church has become lukewarm
There sending so many to Hell

When the preacher preaches the funeral
They preach everyone into heaven
So the family feels good about them
They think if mom or dad made it, they'll make it to

Because people don't know there Bible
They don't know the preacher, can't send you to Heaven
That it's God that will have the last word
The choice is made by how you lived on earth

If we would only stop living for ourselves
Putting God and others before ourselves
We would see a real revival take place
The power of the Lord would then come down

Where do you stand in your walk with the Lord?
Is Christ the center in all you do?
Or are you living close to the edge
Then Christ will have to say depart from me

Your name is not in the book of life
Your name is written in the other book
Of all the things you did to lift yourself up
There is nothing there to allow you in heaven

Written On: 4-22-14

WHO DO WE THINK WE ARE?

Most people love to be asked
Who do you think you are?
Most people think they are great
They'll tell people that, even if they're not

God tells us to choose our words wisely
To say what is only truth
If the words which we say are not truth
Their nothing more than a lie

Many you know, say they love the Lord
Yet their life doesn't measure up
If you don't follow God's Holy Word
You're living nothing more than a lie

Many say they love the Lord
They say they give what's required of them
But bless God I'll not pay my tithes
I don't believe God requires us today

God tells us to bring our first fruits,
Which is a tithe of what we make,
It's a means to show the Lord
That we truly love Him with our whole heart

You're to set the example before the Lord
For His eyes are on all that you do
And if you're obedient to the Lord
He'll bless you in all you do

His Word doesn't tell us
To first pay all our bills
Then put food on the table
And what's left give it to Him

No he tells us to bring our first fruits
Then He'll bless everything that is left
Then if you decide to not obey me
You'll pay them in other ways

It could be your car will break down
Or the house you live in catches fire
You could even lose your job
An you still don't love the Lord

You say that you can't afford to
Pay your tithes on what you receive
The pay check you receive each week
You've not learned to trust the Lord

God who owns everything in the world
Can surely meet all your needs
The ninety percent left, after you pay your tithes
God multiplies it like you've never known

Of course all must be given with a heart of love
Not expecting anything back in return
Then when the Lord knows the desire of your heart
He'll bless you like you've never known

How he blesses the one that pays their tithes
We can't totally explain it to others
But God's multiplication isn't like ours
He blesses in ways impossible for us to explain

Who do we think we are?
To reject God's knocking at our heart?
We tell him to knock at a more convenient time
But we don't know if it could be our last chance

We don't want to give Christ our heart
For we have so much more to do
Things that we desire
Knowing their not pleasing the Lord

God is saying time is running out
My love for you will always stand
But Satan is competing for your life
If you reject me you're yielding to him

God tells us to love our neighbor
Who is that neighbor he's talking about?
Anyone outside your life
He wants us to love all of them

You can't love me if you want
You must love your neighbor here on earth
Loving your neighbor here on earth
When you love them you're loving Christ

Who do we think we are?
If we don't serve the Lord every day
There are so many ways to love him
He'll show us, if we love him with our whole heart

When we truly love the Savior
We'll love spending time with Him each day
Christ will only be number one
Or He'll not be Christ, to you at all

He'll not share Himself with any other
That's why He died to set men free
From the bondage of this world
He died because He loved you and me

If we truly love the Savior
And give Christ our whole heart
We'll spend time communicating with him everyday
Yes will spend much time with Him in prayer

If we truly love the Lord Jesus
Will spend much time in His word
Asking Christ to reveal to us
What we need for each day we live

We'll walk hand and hand with the Savior
Allowing Christ to direct each step we take
Stop taking things into our own hands
It will do nothing but separate us from Him

So make sure when you ask the question,
Who do I think that I am?
That you can truly say, I'm a child of the King
For I walk hand and hand with Him

Written On: 11-1-13

WHEN YOUR OUT OF GOD'S WILL

When you're out of God's will
You'll never receive what's best for your life
For God only knows what's best for you
He gives it a step at a time

We're humans only wanting our way
Will do anything to get it
Most times we make the wrong choices
And trouble stands in the way

We play the lottery every week
Each week we keep buying more
Taking food from our table
Using money to be used to pay our bills

You keep thinking you'll win the big one
That's what Satan wants you to think
When one of millions of people that play it
Your chance to win, is very nil

If you would only obey God's word
Remembering all that we have is the Lord's
He has lent it to us for a while
He expects us to use it wisely

You're out of God's will for your life
When you come to that place in your life
Thinking that everything you own
You did it all on your very own

You're out of God's will when you
Don't surrender your life to Christ
For you're living on the wrong side
And you're headed straight to Hell

If you are a child of the King
Yet you yield to the tactics of Satan
You're out of the will of God
And your certainly displeasing the Lord

For when you mix the ways of the world
With the things God wants you to do
The things of this world will overtake you
If you don't rapidly place it under the blood

No the Lord isn't punishing you
But trying to keep you focused on Him
The Lord knows what's best for you
So you won't destroy your own life

Yes you're out of God's will for your life
When you don't spend time with Him each day
Speaking with God in communion through prayer
The Lord wants you to knock at His door

You might say I don't know how to pray
You might be rough at the very first
For you're not used to talking to God
But talk to Him as He's right by your side

The more you talk to Him each day
You'll be surprised how you learn to talk
Telling Him about every need you have
Then thanking Him for what He's blessed you with

If we don't spend time with Him
Praising Him for all He provides
We'll never have a true relationship with Him
He loves hearing praise come from your lips

Oh yes you are out of God's will
When you fail to read God's Holy Word
For God's word is our road map
We must read it to know what to do

God's word is a living book
You can't read it as other books
For every time that you read it
He'll give you something for the day

If you fail to read the word every day
Pieces will be missing from the puzzle
Then you won't be in the will of God
Because of your neglecting God's Word

God grows our life, according to our will
Are we really hungry, for all he has for us?
If we truly have a hunger for what God gives
He'll give you more, one step at a time

As you apply the word to your life
He'll give you more to apply
For when we apply that truth to our life
He knows we're serious in our walk with Him

How many times have you read the same passage?
Yes you read it time and time again
Never receiving anything from it
You were getting discouraged in your heart

Then you finally got serious before the Lord
When you read the passage one more time
It was like that passage jumped out at you
You finally saw something that inspired you

What made that time different than any other
It was you prepared your heart to receive
The Lord knew He could trust you
To share that truth with others you met

You see God doesn't give unto you
To hoard it, all for yourself
He gives it to share with others
So the word will never become void

When we hold God's word to ourselves
We're totally out of God's will for our life
And God may allow things to come
That will wake us from the stupor were in

The woodshed experience he takes us through
Sometimes it isn't very pleasant to us
If only we had yielded to God in the first place
We wouldn't have to go through the woodshed experience

It's never good to get out of God's will
Won't you stay very close to Christ
You'll find you grow rapidly in your walk with Christ
And you'll be in the will of the Lord

Written On: 10- 7-13

REACHING OUT

There are so many ways each of us
Can reach out, let's take a look
So many reach out to others
In ways which only please themselves

Take a person that is very rich
They reach out to everyone
To purchase what they have
Not caring whom they may hurt

Porn is a big thing today
No matter where you turn
There are books most every where
And the computer is grabbing the eye

They put catchy ads on the computer
Not caring whose eyes they catch
So often they catch the eyes of young people
Who are so easy to persuade

They care nothing about statistics
Which have been reported
That most murders and child molesters
Watched porn most of their life

It starts out with just a peep
Then they reach out with stronger things
Then it becomes an obsession
Your life totally depends on it

Obsession turns to acting out
The thing which you see before you
Before long you end up in jail
And you feel you've done nothing wrong

There are other things which affect many
Such a thing called alcohol
It used to be you could only get it
In bars in the local town

Now most any market and store
Sells alcohol in each of them
Children now find ways to purchase it
We keep making it easier for them

We have no concern for the innocent
As long as we get the money we want
Then when we get that money in our hands
We're not satisfied where we've arrived

It then takes many to deeper things
They're now introduced to drugs
The government won't get involved
Because they are part of the problem

They have all these drug raids
To make you think their doing their job
But instead of destroying the drugs
They put it back out on the market

You'd be surprised if you knew
The people in your neighborhoods
Which are getting rich by those drug raids
We're so blinded to what they're doing

There are so many good ways
We can reach out to those in need
When we see people's needs around us
We can reach out to that soul in need

If they have a true need for food
Or a need to pay a bill
Never give them money to pay it for they
Will probably use it for something else

But take them to the market
Or out to make sure the bill is paid
Then offer the plan of salvation
So they can know the true God you serve

Don't be selfish in reaching out to others
Outside the neighborhood you live in
You can reach out to many more
Through missionaries around the world

You may never go to a foreign land
Yet that doesn't exempt you from being a part
For you can provide the need for others to go
And the souls they reach you have a part

You see God doesn't expect everyone to go
Yet he expects everyone to participate
Know you can't send every missionary
Yet you can support some, who go

So many just give to anyone or thing
Without checking where there money goes
They could be supporting people or programs
Which makes the Lord very unhappy

You may say, what do you mean?
Let's take a much closer look
What part goes to the administration
Never getting to where you desire

Let's take a look at the United Way
A big portion goes to the boy and girl scouts
They support the homosexual ways
Which is strictly against God's Holy Word

If we support such an organization
We've now embraced the things they do
Then this being against God's Holy Word
Could send you straight to Hell

You might say I didn't realize it
If you didn't realize it my friend
If you repent of it today
God will forgive you of all your past

Yet he requires of you to no longer
Support the organization any more
I lost my job at a bank one time
They couldn't brag of 100% support any longer

As a believer you must make the right choices
No matter what the results may be
Remember the Lord is keeping records
What's in his book, means either Heaven or Hell

Won't you desire to make the right choices
By reaching out to the Lord every day
Asking the Lord to help you make the right choices
So your choices will please Him

Written On: 9-30-13

PERSECUTION

When we look at persecution
Nobody loves to go through it
Persecution can overwhelm you
Persecution can cause you to lose your life

Persecution can hurt your pride
If you're not living close to Christ
Persecution can lead you down the wrong path
Then you blame the Lord for it

The Lord said, He'd never
Put anything upon us we couldn't bear
But we must live close to the Lord
For his promises to work

Many think they can live as the world
Then they shake their fist at God
That promise doesn't work for them
Since God promised it in his Word

But those which aren't living close to Christ
Or surrendered their heart to Him
Can't claim any promises of God
The Bible is written for true believers

True believers need to hunger for righteousness
They can't get enough of Christ
They can't fail in seeking God daily
So their life can be truly blessed

When persecution comes their way
God will give them the strength
To face the trials before them
Knowing the test is for them

So they will grow stronger in the Lord
Each time a test comes their way
Yes we can expect many tests in our lives
If we're living close to the Lord

There are reasons God allows them to come
They're not to punish us
But to show the Lord who you trust in
Whether you trust in God, or trust the world

The world will lead you down the wrong road
When self has become your god
God won't share himself with anyone else
For our trust must be totally in Him

Another reason God allows them to come
Is so we can show the world God is real
And we have to look for our answers
By sticking our head in God's Book

Books which man have written
Are written to make us think
But they're not the final answer
For many will lead us astray

We must match them up with God's Word
Asking the Lord to show us the plan
Which He has set forth for us
Then your heart can be truly blessed

God is the way, the truth and the light
If we let him lead the way
Rather than allow our opinion
To dominate our life

That way our life will flourish
We'll grow deeper in the things of God
For we're showing God we love Him
By following God's Holy Word

Not, picking and choosing
Things we desire in God's word
Making excuses for other things
Why we can't follow Christ

Excuses only lead you farther
Away from the love of Christ
Then lead you down the wrong road
Which is leading people to Hell

So when persecution comes to you
Just ask the Lord to lead you through
Asking Him what He wants to teach you
So you can be truly blessed

If you give every trial you face in life
Totally over to the Lord
You'll come out of that trial much faster
Yes each trial will come to an end

So serve the Lord with gladness
Letting Him lead the way
You'll began seeing how rapidly
You start growing, in the things of the Lord

Written On: 6-18-12

A FAMINE

There are famines most everywhere
Most are blinded to their existence
For their so tied up in their self
That they can't see what's happening around them

There have been famines down through the ages
Yet we close our eyes and ears to them
For we don't want to see what's happening
As they've happen over and over again

We seem to not learn from our past
For we think we know more than they did
So don't push history on me
I don't want to hear it from anyone else

I'll make up my own mind
Won't you keep your words to yourself
For I don't want to hear it
That's the thinking of most people

When the word famine is spoken to us
The first thing which comes to our mind
Is when a drought hits a nation
Yes when we fail to get any rain

Because of the rains not coming
The gardens fail to produce
So there's no food to feed the people
And many people end up dead

There's a greater famine in the world today
Which most don't want to talk about
And this famine is so broad today
It extends all around the world

This famine is hitting so many people
Yes, most people upon this earth
Most people don't want to talk about it
They say everything's alright

You find it in most every home
Downtown and the grocery stores
At work, and at play
Yes any place you might mention in life

The sad thing is that you find it
In all churches across the land
God didn't design famine for the church
Yet it is still there any way

It's all because man wants his own way
He doesn't want to follow God's rules
So man ends up living his own life
Then they end up in a real mess

This famine which I'm talking about
Sometimes is intentional
We just don't want to follow God's plans,
Thinking our plans are so much better

When we fail to follow God's blueprints
Life won't be very pleasant for you
For Satan is the one which takes over
And he'll lead you down the wrong path

Remember Satan is a thief and a robber
He'll steal your mind and your soul
He takes you only one step at a time
He's very clever in how he does it

That's why the Holy Spirit, we need to embrace
First to except Christ into our life
If you don't have a zeal to follow the Lord
You haven't given Christ, your all

For once you except Christ into your life
Your mind set will totally change
You'll not get enough of Jesus
You'll keep longing for more of him

If this hasn't happened in your life
You don't have what God has for you
So you need to get back to the alter
And surrender your whole life to Christ

So don't hold back in giving Him your mind
Yes your body, mind, and your soul
For Christ is looking for your whole heart
No, he won't just accept a part

Don't worry about all the bad things
Which you have in your life
The Holy Spirit will deal with you about them
As the Lord leads you along the way

Oh yes there are things people will see right away
Thing's which people will see that you've changed
Then other things the Holy Spirit will tug at your heart
As you keep getting more serious about the Lord

You'll never stop learning things from God
Until the day you take your last breath
So stop beating yourself over your head
Thinking God surely doesn't love you

But as conviction comes to your life
Don't, just push it aside
But quickly ask Christ to forgive you
Be assured Christ will answer your cry

David in the bible made many mistakes
But God always forgave him of them
All because David had a tender heart
Wanting to please the Lord in all he did

Once David asked the Lord to forgive him
He no longer dealt with that sin
So David moved on in his life
Living each day for the Lord

These examples were set in the Bible
Not just for a story to enjoy
But they were placed in the Bible
To help us not get caught up in sin

You see the great famine in the Bible
Is a famine to not seek the Lord
For people, yes people in the church,
Are letting the world reign in their lives

The famine is one where people,
Those which call themselves Christian,
No longer have the zeal in their lives
To hunger and thirst after righteousness

They know longer thirst for righteousness
There are so many things reaching for their soul
And they're allowing the cares of this life
Control their lives each day they live

Yet the cares of this life they're living
Are controlling the life which they live
Things like sports, TV, and electronics
And even most of their vacations

You take your pick at what you do
It consumes the life you're now living
Where Christ is placed on the backburner
Saying if I find time, I'll fit Christ in

Yet God is screaming back to us
I want your whole heart or nothing else
For I am your creator
I want to have your undivided attention

There are all types of help books
And seminars everywhere you go
But there seems to be little concern for God
To teach us how to live our lives on earth

There's a famine to read God's Holy Word
A famine to spend much time in prayer
And bless God just don't expect me
To fast as God's word tells us to do

Sometimes it's the only way we can break
The famine we find ourselves in
We think we can do it on our own
Bless God I'll not miss a meal

So the famine has left us very weak
And vulnerable for Satan to control our lives
You see it's not always the obvious things
That keep us from following Christ

It's doing so many of those good things
Yes of those which we do in the church
Those things control the life we live
Not giving our time to read God's Word, and pray

No, time to meditate on God's Holy Word
You think you have more pressing things to do
That's how Satan will deceive you into Hell
And you'll not realize you're going there

So won't you get your priorities in order?
Start each day spending valuable time with God
Then ask the Lord to give you direction
Then when He gives it, be quick to follow

Don't get caught up in the famine
Sweeping churches and people across this land
For if you get caught up in this famine
Hell will be awaiting you

Written On: 10-1-15

CHOICES

The world is full of choices
Which are both good and bad
How do you fair with your choices
It's so important to your life

Most choices are for ourselves
In order to get what we want
The problem with most of our choices
Most are not God's will for our life

That's why man is in trouble today
And our lives are filled with sin
Everywhere you look my friend
There's murder, theft, and bitterness of heart

Man has put himself first
And left God out of their lives
God said he wants all of us
Or he doesn't want anything at all

Man has become so arrogant
They never think of others around them
Bless God I'm going to do what I want
No one will stop me, not even God

That's when you waver to far
God pulls his Holy Spirit from you
That's when things start going real bad
Not realizing what's happened to you

That is a bad place to be
I'm talking to believers in Christ
When we take on that mentality
We leave Christ out of our life

Without Christ, we will lose out with him
Yes we will lose our salvation
Yes, God will welcome you back
But you've got to turned back to him

It's so hard to get back to the Savior
And most will never return
Satan has sent seven times more imps
To keep you from hearing the voice of God

Now you have only one to blame,
That's yourself, for pushing God away
When God had been so good to you
You once had great fellowship with him

Just where was it you went wrong
When you decided you wanted your way
So rather than listening to the Lord
You turned your life over to Satan

Serving Christ with all your heart
Brings a blessed peace to your soul
The Lord said he would never forsake us
If we put Him first in our life

Yes we will face troubles and trials
That's part of helping us to grow
We face trials just as the world does
But we have God on our side

God allows those trials to come
Just like trials that comes to the world
But when we turn them over to the Lord
They can't stay in our life very long

That trial is allowed to come our way
God knows it will help us grow stronger
If we keep focused on Jesus rather than
The trial which were going through

God knows that we will face trials
He said we will not face ones we can't bare
If we keep focused on Jesus
He'll help us through every one

As those trials that face us each day
They'll help us to grow stronger in the Lord
And God sees greater trials ahead for us
So he allows smaller ones to come first

Those smaller trials which come to us
Are preparation for the greater ones
So stop trying to take things in your own hands
But allow the Holy Spirit to lead you along

When the greater trials come your way
And the world thinks you will fall
God will lift you up through the battles
The battles will become so much smaller

The reason they're not as big to you
You've passed the tests which came first
Now you have much to rejoice over
For the Lord is always on your side

Then the testimony which you now have
Can help so many others along the way
People are looking for someone
Which is a true believer in Christ

God's not looking for wimps
Which say that they love the Lord
And when trials come their way
They start crying like a baby

No, God is looking for warriors
Which will stand strong in the battle
A true warrior for the Lord Jesus Christ
Will make an impact for the Lord

So won't you stand up and be a warrior
In the battle for right and wrong
Stand very strong for Jesus
So he will be proud of you

Then many others will come to the Savior
Because of you being strong in the Lord
Don't give up in the midst of the battle
It could be the last battle you'll have to face

The next place that you will face
Is in heaven for all eternity
So don't give up in the battles you're facing
Don't give up before you take your last breath

Written On: 7-2-14

GIVING YOUR ALL

We hear people every day
Say I will give my all
But when they get down to it
They never give every thing

You go to school each and every day
The teacher sees the progress you've made
These are the words that came out of her mouth
If you would give your all, you'd do much better

You promised the teacher you'd do much better
Yet after you leave the class
You forget the words you promised
For you find so much more to do

You had a recess an hour later
You could do what you wanted to do
If you had only taken that time to study
You would have time to go out that night

But you wasted that time away
Talking to all of your friends
By the time you got out of school
You still had all that extra work to do

Once you got home you went to your room
You thought you would now do that work
But the phone rang and you talk for two hours
Now it was time for supper

After supper you had promised your friends
You would go with them to the mall
You wasted the rest of the evening away
Failing to get that extra work done

Once you went back to school the next day
The teacher was giving a test
Now you failed to pass the test
You hadn't taken time to study

Now it pulls your grades way down
The teacher now talked to you again
She had asked you why you failed the test
When you told her you would give your all

You see the teacher saw the potential you had
If you would learn to apply yourself
There wasn't anything she could do
If you didn't take her advise

You now flunked the class that year
You didn't learn to discipline yourself
You needed that class so badly
In order to move on to the next grade

Now all your friends move on
But you had to stay behind
All because you were not willing
To give your best to your studies

Serving the Lord is about giving
Everything to the dear Lord above
He won't take second place
It's first place or nothing at all

Once you surrender your life to Christ
Then God requires us to turn from the past
Giving Him first place in everything
Not doing those questionable things

You see if those things you're doing
Has a question of whether they're right or wrong
Be assured you better leave them alone
For they will lead you farther from the Lord

Now that you have surrendered to Christ
If you totally meant it from your heart
Yes you are now a child of God
But you must be very careful

For if you don't stay focused on Jesus
You'll start drifting from the Lord
You don't want to be that one
Which falls out of the arms of Christ

Yes Jesus said he'd never leave or forsake us
But there's so many if's along the way
Jesus said if you abide in the vine
You will continue to receive strength from me

But if you waver to far from the fold
My strength will no longer reach you
Then I will sever you from the vine
For you'll know longer be any good to me

So if you are a child of God
Don't mess around with the things of this world
For the things of this world will consume you
Consuming your life from walking with Christ

Those things you're doing may not be bad
But they consume your time each day
Taking your mind off the will of Christ
Weakening you each day that you live

Walking with Jesus is a full time job
Always pleasing the Lord in what you do
What he requires of each of us
Is to give Christ your all in what you do

There's another voice calling out to you
It's the deceiver of your soul
He wants you to listen to him
He'll deceive you to believe everything is alright

Once we yield to his beckoning
He'll take us to places we should never go
At first they'll seem to not be bad
Yes he'll twist your mind to believe in him

Then the world will start looking better
As you yield to the places he takes you
Before long the world will control your life
To where you know longer serve Christ

Where are you standing in God eyes?
Does he see someone passionate for Christ
Or does he see a person
That is drifting each day from the fold

If you find yourself drifting
You better repent and turn back to Christ
For you may find yourself severed from Jesus
And Hell will be your final home

Why not serve Jesus with your whole heart
He'll take you to heights you've never dreamed
And you'll make an impact for Jesus
And heaven will be your final resting place

Written On: 3-24-14

GIVING ALL

We think about the little boy,
In the Bible, that was in the crowd
In which Jesus was teaching them
Yet it begins to get very late

The people had been there all day
And Jesus brought his talk to an end
The disciples wanted to send them home
But Jesus said they would faint on the way

The disciples asked what he would do
He said, have all the people sit down
The disciples then responded to him
There's nothing here to feed all of them

The disciples said, all the food we can find
Was that of a little boy's lunch
He only had five loaves of bread
And two very small fishes

We must understand what happened
This boy was very small
The bread was nothing more than nuggets
And the fishes were nothing but minnows

Jesus asked them to bring him his lunch
Remember we must come as a little child
I'm sure the little boy was hungry
Yet he was willing to give up his lunch

That little boy gave up everything
For he was a follower of Christ
How many of us will give up everything
Not knowing what Christ would do with it

The question each of us would have
Will I give up all I have?
For if I give up all my food
I won't have any for myself

Our self seems to always be
Number one in our life
For our trust isn't totally in Jesus
We haven't allowed our faith to grow

We have the wrong concept of faith
I'll give if I can see
When God says step out and give
Believing God will bless your giving

We think about blessings flowing
Immediately after you respond to Christ
You could be blessed right then
Or much later along in life

No one knows what happened to that boy
But be assured God blessed his life
For when we give everything
God has great things ahead for us

Be assured God met his every need
And be assured he grew in the Lord
Who knows but that many years later
He may have become a great leader

Or he could have become a missionary
In a foreign land to teach God's word
Where many people came to the Lord
Yes, the Savior of the world

Multitudes of people may have come to the Lord
Because of the unselfishness of a boy
You never know where Christ will lead you
And the impact you'll have for Him

The question each must ask ourselves
Am I listening to hear God's voice?
It could come from God's Holy word
As we hunger for all He has for us

You see he cannot speak to your heart
If you don't desire all he has for you
Asking Christ to reveal to you
What he desires for you to do

Then Lord, when I hear you speaking
I'll be willing to following your leading
Applying your truth to my life
So I can be pleasing to you

Then Lord when I hear you speaking
I'll be willing to follow your leading
Applying your truth to my life
So I can be pleasing to you

Not my will but thine be done
Is my cry to you, Dear Lord
For I want to be found faithful
To what you want for my life

Then Lord I know you can speak
In a still small voice to my heart
As I go to sleep at night
Or any time I stop to listen

Then the Lord speaks in other ways
Think of the gifts he's given to you
Sometimes he speaks in services
Through tongues and interpretation

God speaks through older men
Through dreams he gives to them
He sometimes speaks to the younger
Through visions which also he gives

There's no limit to how he speaks
Yet many which he speaks to
Don't take the time to listen
For we've decided to listen to self

Everything we do in this world
After accepting Christ into our life
Everything we do from that time forward
Is to be done to praise the Lord

It's not to lift ourselves up
If we do, God knows we'll fail
For we're not focused on the Lord
Our focus falls on self

Yes this world will start consuming us
And eventually we will fall
For our life isn't totally surrendered
To all the Lord wants to do thru us

Are you giving Christ your all?
Or are you mixing your life with the world?
God says He'll never share himself with anyone
When you do, your life will start drying up

Eventually the world will start taking over
Then you will start losing out with Christ
Won't you stay focused on Heaven
So Christ won't sever you from the vine

As for me and my house
We will serve the Lord
Won't you join in this commitment
So your life won't be cut off, from Christ?

Written On: 3-26-14

FIXING WHAT IS BROKEN

As we live our lives each day
We face so many troubles and trials
Sometimes we look forward to having
Some type of trial every day

That's why many a trial comes
For the Bible plainly tells us
As a man thinketh in his heart
So it shall come to pass

How often have you heard people say?
I know I'm going to fail today
They've already spoken failure
Be assured it will come your way

When each of us should be saying
I can do all things through Christ
The one which strengthens me
I believe it in Jesus Name

When we start with a positive attitude
We can accomplish so much more in life
Negative attitudes prepare us
To be assured of failure in our life

If your attitude is broken
You need to seek the Lord in prayer
Then team up with a positive person
Which believes in positive things

When they help you change your attitude
And you give your life to Christ
That can be the beginning of changes
That will help you advance in life

Some things which are broken
Happen because of our neglectful thinking
We fail to do any maintenance
Knowing it's time to upgrade our life

Like spigots in the kitchen
They're forty years old
Instead of replacing the spigots
You keep on using them

Then three years later they break
Your kitchen has been flooded
Now you have more problems
For you had neglected to fix them

Or how about the car you drive
You've been having problems for months
It's been very hard to start
Then cold weather comes along

You keep cranking the motor over
Now you're sitting in the driveway
You knew you needed a tune up
You just kept putting it off

Now you had to miss work that day
You didn't have a way to get there
So you had to stay home and get it fixed
Along with a hefty tow bill

Well our lives aren't any better
We neglect it almost every day
We eat too much junk food
Then wondering why we're having health problems

There's no nutrition in the food you eat
So your body starts breaking down
You just can't believe you're having problems
It's because you neglect to eat good food

You have just become too busy
To take time to cook a meal
Even to take some good vitamins
You take cheap ones that aren't any good

You get just what you pay for
If you buy cheap, don't expect them to work
For they are designed to do you no good
They don't want then to take away from selling their pills

How about your marriage
You loved each other so much
Yet you neglect to do things together
So you just keep drifting apart

You never do things together
You keep going your own way
Then the other feels neglected
Before long you stop talking

Then someone notices what's happening
And they start moving in on you
Teasing you on how you dress
Or making gestures that excites you

Before long you're asking for a divorce
You're wondering, where did I go wrong
It was all your own fault
Because you failed to maintain your marriage

You thought work was more important
Than spending time with your spouse
You spent so much time at work
You neglected your husband or wife

Then you spent more time at work
With one of the opposite sex
You start drawing closer to them
Then when you were with your husband or wife

Or how about your children
You're so involved in their lives
Taking them to all of their events
Their just involved in too much

So you never spend time with your spouse
Then once the children are gone
You have nothing in common
You just can't seem to pull it together

There are more parents that get divorced
After the children leave the nest
Than any other time in life
You loved your children more than you spouse

Yes we need to truly love our children
But our spouse should be number one
If we want a strong marriage
We need to have a balance in it

How about the life we live
Have we surrendered our life to Christ?
We need to keep in tune with Jesus
So our life will grow in Him

How many people do you know who
Start compromising their salvation with the world
When the Bible teaches He'll share Himself with no other
We must totally trust in the Lord

God has given everyone a will
He'll never force Himself on anyone
So you must decide whether to follow Jesus
Or whether you will follow the world

If you play around with the world to long
God's word tells us, He'll cut us off
Once you're severed from the vine
The vine being Jesus Christ

Once you're severed from the vine
What happens when you're cut from it?
You quickly start drying up
Once dried up, you can't be put back on

If you once accepted Christ into your life
And you find yourself playing with the world
You must repent of the sins you've committed
Before the sins over take you

For no one knows how long Christ will wait
Before He severs you from the vine
You can't be severed from Christ
Unless you once were connected to Him

So stop thinking once you have accepted Christ
In your heart, then you can do what you want
For yes Christ will sever you from Himself
If you don't produce fruit in your life

The closer you draw to the Savior
The happier you will become
Even when trials come your way
He'll walk with you through them

Won't you walk with Christ each day
So your life will be prepared for heaven?
Walking with Christ every day
Is the only way to be assured of Heaven

Written On: 1-9-14

CLASS OF 1965

The class of 1965
Was fifty some years ago
Most haven't ever gotten together
Yes some will never meet again

I just can't fully remember
For things happen with old age
But I think it was a class of thirty one
We were looking to get away from school

Oh yes a few went on to higher learning
To advance their education
But most of us went through
The school of hard knocks

For some you haven't changed much
For others you don't look the same
Some are slim just like before
While others have put on much weight

Most have formed wrinkles here and there
It's nothing to be ashamed of
That's part of just getting old
Yes part of the aging process

Most have children and grandchildren
They come flocking to our doors
There's nothing like those siblings
Which bring joy into our life

But there are always a few
Which are rebellious along the way
Which brings a lot of sorrow to us
Yet we still love them so

Most of our teachers in the school
Which we had when we were there
Have passed on or are up in years
Remember we are now the old ones

There was nothing like that Flintstone School,
Which stood firmly in the mountains,
It was a school we could be proud of
Even though the high school is no longer there

Yet memories are still in our minds
Of the good ole times we spent there
Many say they would like to turn the clock back
Not me, I'm longing for Heaven

We've gone through all those years
We've had hard times along with good
Yet it's all about how we processed them
Whether we're better on the other side

Everyone will never meet again
For life will eventually end for us
The question is, has your life counted
To be with the Lord up in Heaven

We can all have a reunion up there
If we surrender are all to Christ
And live for Christ everyday
So that when we take our last breath

God will say to each one which served
Christ with their whole heart
Welcome home to Heaven
For you are now a child of mine

None wants to hear those dreadful words
Depart from me I never knew you
Won't you get your house in order
Preparing for eternity?

Written On: 7-5-15

GIVE IT AWAY

Giving something away
Is something which will thrill your soul
If done in the name of Jesus
Your life will change to glorify Christ

As you give things away as a little child
It gets embedded in your soul
You feel the joy that starts flowing
When you don't expect anything in return

If you expect something back
You really haven't given it away
You have only become an Indian giver
Not realizing the principle of giving

When you're taught to give ten percent
Of your money to God above
It's a command by God in heaven
And we must learn to give in love

When we learn the principle of giving
Along with the principle of love
Be assured that God will bless your life
God blesses those which learn to give

As a young adult you learn to give
Yes you give your life away to another
In the bond of marriage you say your vows
It's not a contract but a covenant

That's when real life begins for you
Yes for both you and your spouse
When you put Christ first in your life
And you learn to work differences out

Most young people look at it differently
If it doesn't work out I will leave
Not realizing it is a covenant of God
Those trials will help you grow stronger

It's not all about yourself
But what I can give, to the other
That's what makes a marriage stronger
Living God's way, and not for myself

But the most important thing you can do
Is be obedient to the Lord
Seeking all he requires of me
And to follow his leading each day

The first thing we need to do
Is give our life totally to Christ
Without this first step in our life
You can't fully be blessed

For blessings truly come from God above
Why shouldn't we love Him
Remember God owns the cattle on every hill
And the wealth in every mine

In other words, He owns everything
He loans it to us for a while
And when our life on earth ends
He'll take it back to share with another

It's important to give the gospel away
To the lost wherever we go
So they too can share the good news
After they have excepted Christ in there heart

Have you learned to give my friend?
Giving is not just monetary things
But giving the love of Jesus to others
By how you react and how you smile

Won't you embrace the love of Jesus
Serve Christ the rest of your life
So you'll enjoy the life that you live
And make life grand for those around you

Written On: 7-12-15

I'M NOT THE MAN I USED TO BE

Have you stopped to analyze
Where you once were, and where you are today
As a true believer in Jesus Christ
Which you say you are

We need to take inventory of our life
As business men take so often
If you never take inventory of your life
You'll never know where you stand in Christ

Too many live their life day by day
Nothing ever changes in their life
And in the process of each day
They embrace bits of the world

If you don't take daily inventory
Of the life in which you live
You'll never know how far you've drifted
From where you used to be in the Lord

The Bible plainly teaches each of us
If we truly want Heaven to be our home
We must accept Christ into our heart
That's our ticket to get to Heaven

After accepting Christ into our life
We must turn our back, on our old life style
And embrace Jesus each and everyday
Loving Jesus with our whole heart

Wanting all he has for us
Not seeing how close, I can get to the edge
For if that's the mentality that we have
We've never embraced Jesus in our heart

Then once we've started the Christian walk
We must pray to God each day
In the name of Jesus
It's the only way to get to the Heavenly Father

The Bible plainly tells us
There's only one way to God above
That's through the name of Jesus
That's why Jesus obediently went to the Cross

Death could not hold him down
After being placed in that sealed tomb
On the third day he rose again
Yes death couldn't hold him down

Jesus now holds the key to heaven
We must go to God in Jesus Name
When we do, the portals of heaven
Will swing open wide for us to enter in

God holds nothing back from us
Yes he gave us his Holy Word
It was written as God inspired the hearts of men
To write it down for our road map

The Word is truth, from beginning to end
No one can change its truth you see
Yes people say God's word is contradictable
But they haven't read the word in context

They take bits and pieces of it
And say it contradicts other scriptures
But much of what we believe
Is contingent on other passages

So if the Word seems to contradict other scriptures
You're missing something in God's word
For God says were not to take from
Or add to His Holy Word

The puzzle of God's Holy Word
Fits together if we search it out
God's given us each a will
He'll never force it on our lives

We must accept God's Word by faith
His word can wipe stumbling blocks away
If we truly embrace God's Holy Word
It has true food for each and every soul

Yes the hunger you have from deep within
God will meet that hunger down in your soul
If you embrace Jesus with all your heart
And turn your old life over to him

That's all our soul ever longs for
All we must do is reach out and receive
But the things in which we reach out for
Must be according to God's Holy Word

God's word says he'll give us the desire of our heart
If we truly love the Lord, with everything with in
For the only things we will ask for
Are things which are pleasing to the Lord

I can say from deep down in my soul
I'm not the man which I used to be
I know longer embrace the things of the world
Not even church, denominations, and friends

Don't get me wrong, yes they are important
But too many put their trust in them
Rather than embrace the Lord of our soul
They'll lead you astray from the Lord Jesus Christ

You'll get caught up in all types of programs
Without putting Christ in the center of them
Then you're more interested in building a big church
Rather than feeding souls with the word

Then you get caught up in those programs
Jesus can't speak to your soul
Then you become lukewarm in your life
And if you stay there to long, God will cut you off

I've come to that place in my life
Yes I belong to a local church
For Christ set the church in order
It's not set to do our own thing

Yet every denomination has their good points
So I listen to each of them
I embrace the things which measure up
To God's word, and cast the others aside

Yes I try and weigh out what is spoken
The rest I cast aside for I don't want
To corrupt my mind and my soul
So my life will be pure and clean

I don't want churches, and denominations to corrupt me
But too many put their trust in them
Rather than embrace the Lord of our soul
Many will lead you away from the cross

They get caught up in all types of programs
Without Christ the center of them
They're more interested in building a big church
Rather than teaching and reaching souls

They're so caught up in all those programs
Jesus can't speak to their soul
They become lukewarm in their life
And if they stay there to long, Christ will cut them off

I don't want to live upon this earth
Trying to please man in all that I do
For man doesn't have the ticket to heaven
They'll lead you straight to hell

It's important to keep focused on Jesus
Taking an inventory of our life each day
If you should waver from the things of God
Quickly repent of the wrong you've done

You can be a true believer
Serving Christ through your whole life
But because you didn't take inventory
You found out you've drifted for many years

Then when you face, the Lord above
God can't use you in his kingdom
Some say that it's impossible
In that parable, God's speaking to believers

He says if we don't produce
He'll sever us from the vine
The vine being the Lord Jesus Christ
What a terrible place for us to end

We need to daily take inventory of our life
So we'll know if were starting to drift
Quickly repent and get back on track
Before you end up going too far

Written On: 11-4-13

CHARITY

The good ole USA
Was the greatest nation on earth
We reached out to people around the world
Helping them with all their problems

When someone or nation got in trouble
We seemed to always be the first one to respond
For God was the head of this great nation
And we also loved Israel so much

As long as we blessed Israel
Our nation was oh so prosperous
Along with individual people
God said, He'd bless those who blessed Israel

As time has passed along
We have let our guard down
Forgetting who was ahead of this nation
It was God which has brought us together

Our separation from God started early
Satan has taken his time destroying us
Remember Satan is a deceiver
When he loses a battle, he doesn't give up

When most Christians win a battle
They spend so much time rejoicing
They spend too much of their time rejoicing
Over what they have just accomplished

That's exactly where Satan wants you
That's when he'll slip a little teaser in
It may not seem like much to you
But that's how Satan works in people's lives

He places a big law before us
Which he knows won't be passed
To get people all aroused with it
So we forget what's happening behind the scene

He's used this trick throughout time
Just think of all the laws he's crammed through
Once he gets all those little laws passed
Putting them together they become the big law

All the time when we were rejoicing
Satan never ever missed a beat
Yet you were deceived into believing
That those little laws would be alright

All those ungodly laws which have been passed
In our congress which is supposed to serve us
Yes even approved by our presidents
Yes leaders of this great nation

People have now become numb
To God's plan for this great nation
People are no longer sensitive to God's Word
It's all about self and not about God

We were a nation sending missionary's
All around the world, so all could hear
Fulfilling what God's word declared
Before the end, the gospel would be in all nations

That every nation would hear the gospel
That was a promise sent to us by God
Today we can say that all nations
Have received the good news of God's word

You may say what has this to do with charity
It has so much to do with it my friend
Because along with spreading the gospel
Charity is what financed the gospel

We showed love to people and nations
Then they were more open to receive God's word
It was the charity of loving people
Which financed the gospel around the world

The one world order is about to be ushered in
How do I know, let's take a look
There few prophecies which hasn't been fulfilled
Which would stop the Lord from returning

Their passing laws everyday
So rapidly we can't track them
Cramming them in with good bills
Not being read by our lawmakers

An example is the hate crime bill
Who wouldn't pass a law for hate?
But we already had laws to cover hate
They had another thing in mind

The hate crime bill was pushed by the Muslim's
They had an agenda in mind
To shut the voice of Christians
To not spread the gospel around the world

Without the good news of the gospel
They could spread the news of the Muslim faith
No their message is not of God
For they don't love all people

Their message is to kill all people
Which don't belong to their religion
Christians and Jews are their number one goal
For they bring shame to their god Allah

Once the Christian's voice has been stopped
It will be easy to usher the one world order in
Which will happen after the rapture takes place
When Christians are raptured from this earth

All the laws of this present administration
God has let them do as they wished
Also blinding the eyes of the Republicans
To pass all the ungodly laws against God

With every administration of the past
They couldn't pass all these ungodly laws
The Lord wouldn't allow it until the present time
For it wasn't time for the end to come

But this present president hates the Lord
Along with his administration that's under him
Now we can say he isn't a Christian
Because God's word says we will know them by their fruit

The only fruit in which their portraying
Is fruit coming from Hell itself
Preparing to usher in the one world order
When Christians leave this earth

He hates all believers around the world
And God's chosen people the Jew's
So the one in which he is following
Is Satan which is the deceiver of this world

They've gone so far that marriage isn't sacred
Abortions for baby parts is a daily thing
There's no remorse for either one
For their hearts are numbed by the devil

God's allowed this all to come to pass
For they have drifted to far from Him
Most will never ever find the Lord
Their heart and soul has no love for Him

They even want to stop charity
By paying what we give to the government
So they can disburse it to whoever they want
So they can promote the works of Satan

So many in the world has been caught in this trap
For their lives no longer focus on the Lord
The creator of this great universe
Which He made a plan for us to escape

But no, were not interested in God's plan
In our lives we're only thinking about self
So forget about charity in our lives
Let's grab everything for our self

What we have forgotten is that God above
Blesses us according to our giving
Giving is more than just ten percent
It's about giving our whole self away

Many say they have given their self away
Yet there's hidden things they want to keep
So God can't help them, because they have lied
By holding back what they said they had given

Let's stop lying to God up in Heaven
He already knows everything
All we're doing is heaping coals of fire on our life
Preparing our lives to be sent straight to Hell

So remember charity is a good thing
We're to give till we take our last breath
God has only leant it to us for awhile
Were to do what the bible requires

Give our whole self, our time, our talents
The money which He loaned to us
God will bless you more than you'll ever know
So get on board to learn what giving is about

Written On: 9-1-15

TO WHOM OR WHAT ARE YOU SEEKING?

As we live our life each day
So much seems to be required of us
So often we are totally confused
For there's so many choices in life

The choices which we make each day
Seem to daily multiply
It makes it so hard for us all
Yet there's only one right choice

You could be going to a birthday party
There were going to be many there
You know some of the things which they like
Aren't appropriate for you

Will they really use it?
Or will they stash it away
What kept pondering in your mind
Will they really use it or not

Waiting on the Lord each day
Should be the first step we make
Life would be so much pleasant
If we would only let God lead the way

But no, we think that we have
Much better things in mind
So we make our own choices
Rather than let God lead the way

The Holy Spirit could be speaking
To our lives we live each day
He doesn't want to overpower us
So he speaks in a still small voice

That still small voice keeps speaking to you
Each and every day
Yet the things which you do each day
Seem to drown God's voice right out

The things you're doing may not seem bad
Yet they seem to consume your life
So you don't have much time for Jesus
Yes, you're pushing the Lord out

You spend so little time with the Lord
Just an hour or two each week
An once you leave the doors of the church
You close Jesus out of your life

You have so much you want to do
You don't have time to pray
Nor to read God's Holy Word
Things have taken control of your life

You start doing things you love to do
They seem to fill the voids in your life
Yet shortly after they filled that void
There seems to be a great let down

The reason we get so many let downs
We haven't made Christ number one in our life
The world is consuming us each day
Not caring who you've become

Yet God up above sent his only Son
To earth to die for you and me
No other sacrifice would ever do
It was the only perfect sacrifice to be found

So if your life is totally cluttered
Only you can change everything
Stop letting others dictate to you
What's the next thing you'll do in your life?

Put Christ first, in all you do
Then prioritize everything else you do
And you'll be surprised what you can accomplish
You'll have more time than you'll ever believe

You'll stop filling your day with wasteful things
We waste so many minutes every day
Your life will then become so fulfilled
You'll be happy you made those choices

Written On: 12-27-14

WE WIN

You may say, how do we win?
Everyone loves to win
Anytime we win on earth
It puts zeal in our heart

We'll desire to do much more
Then we ever did before
Just take a look at sports
And you can see what I'm talking about

When your winning streak gets stronger
You just don't want to lose a game
Yet there's more to life than winning
In each game we win on earth

Things are so much better
When we lose now and then
Yet with so many people
That's when we leave our guard down

Yes, we all love to win
But what makes losing so important
It's when we lose a game
We need to analyze where we went wrong

Losing is an attitude of the mind
How will I react to what just happened?
Will I look at it as a tragedy?
Or will I lift my head up high

Saying I want to improve my self
Because of mistakes I have made?
So when I play the next game
I'll be so much better

Not to make the same mistakes
Over and over again
But I'll do so much better
Letting the Lord lead the way

When we understand whom we should serve
Our life will improve more and more
Yes, you will still make mistakes
You'll quickly repent of the wrongs you've done

By improving the game you're playing
You'll win more games by improving your game
Then people will begin taking notice
What a great guy you have become

Serving Jesus is much like
The game you play in this life
Yet the games you play in this life
Are mainly played for yourself

Serving Jesus is so much different
We serve Christ to serve Him
Self we must set aside
In order to win the battle were in

You see the battle for Christ is
A battle against good and evil
We fight the battle here on earth
Not to please us, but to please the Lord

For the battles we fight every day
Satan doesn't want you to fight
But to give into his tactics
So you will end up in Hell

Yet God has a much better plan
He wants you to go to heaven
Then live for eternity
Your life will never end

Yet he'll never force himself on anyone
To serve Him my friend
The choice is in our own hands
The choice to live for Christ or the devil

The way to have a great hereafter
Is follow God's road map the Bible
But the Lord's the one keeping records
Our life right now, determines our destination

For when we meet the Lord above
Yes everyone will have to face God
It's the Life which we live on earth
That will be flashed before our eyes

And if the life we've lived on earth
Doesn't measure up to God's Holy Word
We've made our own here after
God will not send you to Hell

You make your choice while living here
Upon this earth my dear friend
The choice is totally in your hands
As where you'll spend eternity

The greatest advice anyone can give you
Is repent of your sins today
Don't put it off any longer
We can't be sure what tomorrow holds

If you chose to repent of your sins
And turn from the past life you've lived
God has made a great promise to us
He'll wipe all past sins away

We're not to go back in our old life style
We're to put on the armor of God
So when Satan comes against you
The Holy Spirit will be by your side

So when you're feeling the tugging at your heart
We need to turn to His leading
So when we fall along the way
Quickly repent and change direction

If we daily read God's Holy Word
Asking the Holy Spirit to lead each step we take
Giving unto us what you need for that day
Be assured the Lord will not lead you astray

Spend time before Him every day
Be assured He'll never lead you astray
And when your life on earth is complete
Be assured you'll be welcomed into Heaven

It's then you can say I won
The battle against good and evil
So the choice is totally in your hands
Won't you give Christ, your whole life today?

Written On: 10-27-15

THE FLAG

The old flag was given to us
Yes the stars are so significant
For the stars represents
Each state which formed this nation

Yet it goes so much farther
It represents the heavens above
Where God is preparing a place
For those which serve Him

Then the strips on that old flag
Also have a significance
They represent the thirteen colonies
Yes people which have the same mind set

The strips have a greater significance
For people which love the Lord
For Christ shed his blood on Calvary
For people to be set free

It was so important to the men that came
From countries a far off
They didn't have freedom
In countries where they had come from

In the countries where they left
They were told how to worship God
But the worship which they were allowed
Was a worship, to squeeze the Lord out

These people loved the Savior
They were willing to die for Him
So they got on these great big boats
Set sail for the unknown

Believing that they would find a place
Where they could worship the Lord freely
Even if they might lose their life
They did it so you and I could be set free

This is the very thing that our Savior did
When Christ went to Calvary
He was willing to die for you and I
Not caring what man might say

But Christ knew that the finished work
Of His death, burial and raising again
Would be the greatest sacrifice
So many in this world could be set free

What a sacrifice of the father
To give his son for you and I today
It's time we get back to the Bible
To preserve what God did for you and me

Satan is trying to destroy this nation
Through men and women which don't care about life
All their looking for is to have a thrill for themselves
Not caring what the final results will be

You see Satan is a deceiver
He wants to destroy every soul he can
For he knows his days are limited
He's destroying as many as he can

Then he knows that when the Lord comes back
Taking with him, those which served him
Then he'll be thrown into the pit of Hell
Along with all whom he has deceived

You see Satan doesn't care who he hurts
He has no love for you and me
He's just mad that he lost the battle
When he tried to take over heaven

Of course, the Lord won the battle
So Satan's days on earth are limited
Most all of the prophesies in the Bible
Have been fulfilled, yet men's eyes are blinded

God's word declares that he will come
At a time when people aren't looking for Him
Yes He will come as a thief in the night
All who don't serve Christ, will be left behind

It will be a dreadful day for you
If you should be left behind
To be left with all the imps of Satan
To destroy your life even more

Yes the Bible has proven itself
Over and over again
Yet people refuse to follow the Lord
Saying, I'll put it off until another time

If that is your mentality
You'll probably be one of those left behind
For you're not heeding God's warnings
To not fool around with our soul

The days are clicking by rapidly
Yes old glory is waving for you and me
Contrary to what the world may say
This nation was birthed for nations to see

We have been the greatest nation in the world
For we were a dear friend of Israel
God said anyone that embraces Israel
He would bless them abundantly

So we have been blessed for many years
The most current administration hates them
And God has been giving us many warning
To get back to the foot of the Cross

The world is preparing for a one world order
Not caring about souls on this earth
And they're about to get what they want
Yes, the rapture is about to take place

God is slowly drawing his Holy Spirit away
From what once was a powerful nation
Won't you look up to that flag that's flying
And remember that this nation was formed by God

Yes, those stars and stripes have flown high
To show the world that we could be set free
Won't you take on the mind of Christ
And let your life shine for Christ today

Remember Christ is coming very soon
Yes time is running out my friend
It's time to embrace the Lord Jesus Christ
Repenting and turning to Him

We that are living in this nation
Which say that we are Christian
Need to start living like we are one
Rather than hiding behind the name

Respecting the old Flag
Which has flown over this nation for years
End this life on a high note
Serving Jesus to the fullest

Written On:2-19-15

THE BIBLE

The Bible is a perfect book
Which has us totally in mind
You can't read it as other books
For there are hidden niches in it

They are only revealed to those
Which have surrendered their life to Christ
And believe the Word is Holy
So you hunger to find what God has for you

He doesn't give you everything
All at once in your life
Only when your life is prepared
To receive it, to share it with others

You see God will not waste his time
With those just playing around
He's looking for those who mean business
For they'll love him with their whole heart

Those which only play around,
Going to church when they please,
Are a hindrance to the work of God
For they're only lukewarm

The Lord can only use committed people
For they will work for the Kingdom of God
Reaching out to see others
Come to the Lord Jesus Christ

People say they could never do things
In the church where they attend
But you'll never know if you can
Unless you give it a try

Many a person in the church
You wouldn't think would amount to anything
But when they become faithful in little things
The Lord promotes them to greater things

As they use the talents God gave them
The Lord adds other talents to them
For He knows He can count on them
To accomplish what God gives them to do

You see God's not looking for talents
He's looking for faithful people
Which will yield to God with their whole heart
For faithful people will get the job done

There are many people in the Church today
God would love to be able to use
But God cannot use them
For there unfaithful in all they do

Most people which say they can't do things
In the church they attend
The reason for those excuses are
If they commit, they'll have to give up other things

They think the things they do are more important
Than serving the Lord with their whole heart
So most which keep making excuses
Will end up in the pit of Hell

Won't you get into the Holy Book
And start following what he has planned
It's then the Lord will reveal to you
Things many others will never see in God's Word

The Bible is so important
It's been proven down through the ages
It's the only book that's total truth
And the Bible never lies

Prophecy's which were spoken
Hundreds of years before they came to pass
Then at the proper time
God's Word finally was fulfilled

No one can find anything
In God's Holy Word
Which has not been fulfilled
Unless the time has not come yet

You must take a look at the prophecies
Which the prophets have proclaimed
To see when the time was
For the prophecy to be fulfilled

No other book is so precious
Which proves God's Holy Word
Won't you get on board my friend
And let Jesus reign supreme in you

Then when this life is over
And your work on earth is done
The Lord will welcome you with open arms
And say welcome home, come on in

Written On: 12-2-11

SO MANY IF'S

It comes up so often
In our life we live today
Let's take a look at what it means
It can help us along the way

It depends on a condition
It depends on something else
So we can't take it as a whole truth
By continuing in our own way

All through the Bible
You read these words "if you"
Do certain things in your life and
These things will, or won't happen to you

These things can be good or bad
Depending on how we respond
So when you read the "ifs" in the Bible
You need to take notice, what the "if" is for

In our everyday walk with Christ
We tell our wife we'll go with her
To church on Sunday
If we get our work done

What we need to realize
It's not our choice to do
God's Word tells us so plainly
To worship the Lord on the Sabbath day

You put that "if" before your wife
Really knowing it wouldn't get done
You might pull the wool over your wife's eyes
But you can't pull it over the Lord

You make a promise to the pastor
You will read your bible every day
That promise is not to the pastor
But that promise is to the Lord

The Bible tells us to study God's Word
To show ourselves approved unto God
That we should never make a vow
Unless we follow through with it

The Bible teaches us so plainly
That we're not to make a vow
Unless we can follow through with it
If we fail, we have sinned

At the place in which we work each day
Our boss has a job for us to do
When we were hired with them
Telling them we would be there best employee

After we were hired by them
We did our best till, after the probation time
Then we decided things were too hard
So we give the employer a fit

We decide we will only do
What we want to do
If the boss doesn't like it
I will take the boss to court

Or you will only work for an employer
If the company has a union
For you know you can goof off
And the union will back you up

Unions believe that everyone
Should be given the same wage
Even if you're a goof off
You should still be rewarded the same

But God looks at it much differently
If you don't work, you don't eat
He doesn't require the same from everyone
He only requires your best

So all that he requires of you
Is do all that you can do
And he will reward us graciously
If we always put our best foot forward

This follows us through every phase of life
Were to take notice of all those "if's"
If we never understand them
We will lose out in life

God's word tells us so plainly
If we surrender our heart to Christ
And believe it from deep in our heart
We can become a child of God

If we walk in the light
As he is in the light
We have fellowship with one another
And Jesus blood cleanses us from sin

If we confess our sins
He's faithful and just to forgive us
And cleanse us from all unrighteousness
Yes, this is written in God's Word

If we say we have no sin
We make God a liar
He makes it very clear
His Word is not in us

We as a husband of the house
Yes a believer in God's word
Tells our wife or our children
I'll give you certain things "if"

That if, which you place before them
Doesn't measure up to God's word
So they're not required of it
Because God's Word tells us otherwise

We tell our children if they
Get certain work done that day
That they will be able to go
With the neighbor the next day

But you goof off and don't get the work done
The "if" was not completed
So when dad or mom saw it wasn't completed
You weren't allowed to go with the neighbor

The question is, do you understand the "if"
There are consequences if you don't follow through
We need to come with our ears open
Listening intensively to God's Holy Word

We can only reach Heaven
If we follow the plan of salvation
Then put God's Word into action
It shows we're serious in walking with Christ

You will not make heaven
By serving any other god
Jesus is the way, the truth and the life
Without Christ you'll not make it to Heaven

Will you surrender to Christ today?
Meaning it from the depth of your heart
By serving Christ the rest of your life
You can then be assured of Heaven

So take notice of all of the "ifs" in the Bible
They're there to warn us of something
Then follow what the Bible teaches you
And God will be well pleased with you

Written On: 3-10-14

SELF CONTROL

So many in the world today
Have no clue what self-control is
They've bought into the political correctness
So there's no laws they can't break legally

They think that they can do
Whatever they want to do
They don't care who they hurt
As long as they feel good about themselves

The problem is, it will catch up with you
As you keep taking advantage of others
When you do these things long enough
You could end up, in jail

The world and nations are headed
Down the road to a one world order
So they must destroy any nation
That supports the God of all nations

Talking about the Father, Son, and Holy Spirit
Which is in heaven looking out for us
Yes there is a Heaven and Hell
At the end which will you enter

You might say, what's this have to do with
Self-control in the life we live?
It is so important to each of us
To not get caught up in the world

The world will try everything they can
To cause you to stumble an fall
But the Lord is beckoning to each of us
Don't cave into all the world's lies

Follow me each day that you live
Don't waver in your walk with Christ
Live the word, out in your life
But do all in kindness and love

Don't bow down to all of their tactics
Make Christ number one in your life
Making the choice even if I should die
I'll follow Christ all the way

The world, yes they can kill the body
It may not be pleasant you see
But the Lord's hand is upon you
Saying I'll go with you through it

Yes the Lord is alive and well
He'll always be by your side
Your life upon this earth my friend
Is very short compared to eternity

So put into practice every day
What living for Christ is all about
Putting into practice every day
Self-control when they come against you

Let people know this is not your home
You have a better place waiting for you
Yes they may mangle or kill your body
But be assured they can't kill your soul

But those left behind in this world
Will not have peace and rest
Until they surrender to the Lord
Giving Christ first place in their life

But if you should keep living your life
As the world would have you do
Be assured you'll not make it to Heaven
You will be sent straight to Hell

Yes there is a Heaven and Hell
Hell is designed for those which haven't surrender to Christ
You say I'll be with all my friends
But be assured you'll be standing alone

Remembering the times you heard a salvation message?
The times you were asked to surrender to Christ?
You'll remember all the times you pushed Christ away
Saying I'll live for Christ some other day

Yet that other day never came
For the noise of the world drowned Christ out
As he knocked at your hearts door
You thought you had more important things to do

Life as we know it today
Keeps passing by very rapidly
And it could be you will be taken prematurely
By an accident or a dreadful disease

You never once thought about Jesus
Satan planted the things of this world in your mind
Even when you went to church on Sunday
You no longer heard the voice of God speaking to you

Your mind was filled with what you would do
Once the service finally came to an end
So going to church did you no good
Other than make you feel good for another week

Always remember eternity is a long time
So long that it will never end
What you do for Christ upon this earth
Will determine whether you'll go to Heaven or not

No doing good things or joining the church
Being baptized in water or many are sprinkled
Being filled with the Holy Spirit
Or coming to church every service

Reading your Bible every day
And spending time in prayer each day
Not one of those things will send you to Heaven
For all of them are portraying works

Oh yes, Christ requires us to do all of them
But not one of them will send you to Heaven
For there's only one way God's Word tells us
That's to repent and turn from your sins

You can't get a ticket to Heaven
Through your parents or living in America
God's Word tells us, we must be covered by his blood
And surrender our whole life to Him

Then once we surrender all to Jesus
Our desires to follow Christ will be there
And if that desire does not come
Be assured you're not totally surrendered to Him

Self-control is also in the equation
You want to treat others around you in love
The question each must ask himself
Has that total change happened to me?

If not, won't you make it your day
That you surrender your whole life to Christ
That's why he died, was buried, and rose again
He made the way for us, but it's our choice

So the choice is in your hands today
Christ would never send you to Hell
It's only you that can send yourself there
By not surrendering, and turning from the world

Written On: 3-18-14

WHAT DOES GOD REQUIRE OF ME?

What does God require of me?
To many it will be a surprise
What he requires of each of us
It's ALL, meaning everything in our life

God must be number one
Ninety nine percent isn't enough
For when you give one percent away
You don't have Jesus fully in your heart

When you give Him your all
He'll multiply things in your life
In ways you can't understand
He desires for you to not stand alone

When you give up one percent
You're giving Satan a place in your life
Your life will never, be fulfilled
Until you give Christ your all

No it may not seem right to you
But God's the creator of our soul
So he's looking out for your best
So be assured your All is what he wants

God requires of us to spend much time
Communicating with Him each day
Yes communicating with Him in prayer
And be serious as we speak to Him

When we're serious he will hear us
When we pray according to God's will
For if we're not giving Him everything
He will not desire to please us

God will provide abundantly
He wants you to enjoy the things he provides
If we try getting ahead of God's will
We will not enjoy what he allows us to have

When we go back to the parable
Where God gave each a different amount
He gave each according to their abilities
No he didn't give them more than they could process

Even though God could have given each more
He knew they couldn't handle it
We must first produce with what he gives
As we prove ourselves, he'll give us more

Stop trying to get your own way
Allow him to guide each step you take
Then you'll be in God's perfect will
You'll be so happy in all you do

God always knows, what is best for us
Stop trying to keep up with your neighbor
Or your friends that you rub shoulders with
As you live your life each day on earth

God requires us to read His Holy Word
It's the road map for our lives
We must read it, to understand it
Where he wants to take us each day

Don't just read it to say, I've read it
So I can now do what I want
But ask God before you read it
To reveal to you, what he has for your life

He requires us to be found faithful
That's what he requires for our lives
And if we should stumble and fall
We need to quickly ask God for forgiveness

All because we want to measure up
To all requirements, He expects of me
When you desire God's will for your life
Your life will advance in God's will

The will of God is so precious
He would never lead us astray
For He longs for sweet fellowship with us
Knowing when we yield totally to Him

We'll have such a loving life
We'll long to love the unlovable
For God loves the unlovable
Through people like you and me

When true love flows out of our life
Into lives which don't love Christ
You'll make an impact in their lives
In ways you think are impossible

The reason God placed us on this earth
Is to love everyone that we meet
And then it is up to the Lord
To draw them unto the Cross

Many a person hasn't come to Christ
Because we have failed to pray
That God would soften their heart
So you can now speak, as the door is opened

So stop trying to do things on your own
Bath each and every day in prayer
And you'll be surprised, what God does through you
As you allow Christ to lead you each day

Written On: 11-11-13

SALT AND LIGHT, PEPPER AND DARKNESS

Who would think these go together
That each can teach us much
To help us live our lives on earth
In a way pleasing to the Lord

God's word is our great teacher
It's designed to make us stop and think
As how we are to live our lives
So we'll bring glory to the Lord

It was said by a pastor years ago
By one which is now deceased
I believe his name was John W. McGee
It's a powerful word to receive

He said that God didn't talk about giraffes
He taught about feeding the sheep
For if he put our food in the air
Most would end up with no food to eat

Not only is this a natural food principle
We can also take it as biblical
Let's take a look at a biblical truth
That can help each of us in life

If God had written His Holy Word
Far above what man could comprehend
No one would make it to heaven
Everyone would end up in Hell

But God wrote His word for everyone
Sending His Holy Spirit to help us along
So if we spend much time in His word
He'll show us what salt is about

Salt when used at the table
Makes our food taste so much better
As it spreads throughout the foods we eat
It bring much pleasure as we eat our meal

Well the word of God is our spiritual salt
It brings so much joy to our lives
But only if we apply it to our lives
Can we enjoy the flavor in it

Will never make an impact wherever we go
If we don't apply God's word to our lives
The word is spread through people like you and me
Won't you apply the truth to all those around you

Salt can be applied wherever we go
Even in the work place where Christ is forbidden
You may say, how can we spread it there?
By living a life pure before them

Not taking part in unethical things
Refuse to do things which may hurt another
Or do things that go against God's Holy Word
Just be that light which shines so brightly

Then pepper represents darkness
Which is the life Satan wants you to live
And as long as he keeps you in darkness
You'll never learn what salt is about

You don't have to look for darkness
No, people don't have to do anything
For everyone is born in darkness
Everyone needs the Savior above

God's Word says there's many on the broad road
Which leads to that terrible place
And God's word tells us so plainly
That most people are on that road

Don't believe all of those preachers
That people are coming to Christ by the droves
Because if we believe all those preachers
Most people would be on the narrow road

And if all those people were on the narrow road
This world would be a more pleasant place
This world would be run by Christians
And our laws wouldn't point to the world

Just listen to all of those preachers
When they preach the funeral of those deceased
They tend to place everyone in heaven
People love to hear those sweet words

By telling all of those people
That they're going to heaven above
They're confusing the minds of many people
For they knew the life which they lived

It's not our job to say where they're going
Judgment is up to the Lord
It's time we point the ones left behind
To the Savior up in Heaven

It has all to do with how, we've lived on earth
And whether we've surrendered our heart to Christ
Are we one which repeated the sinner's prayer
Then lived our life like the devil?

They'll be a lot of good people in Hell
Which have never totally surrendered to Christ
Won't you make that most important step
Then serve Christ with your whole heart

You haven't got time to keep playing around
No one has a guarantee of tomorrow
Why take the chance when you can now choose
Whether you go to Heaven or Hell

Sin is not always a visible thing
Which we see with our naked eye
Sin can be nothing more than neglect
Which keeps piling up in your life

Even a true believer
Needs to daily repent of their sins
You don't want to be caught with sin in your life
When Jesus comes or you go by death

Won't you surrender all to Jesus
Allowing Christ to direct your life
So when the rapture or death comes to you
You'll be ready to go to heaven

Written On: 9-2-15

WHAT ARE YOU HEARING?

Our minds are so cluttered today
We hear too many voices
What voice are you hearing today?
Is it the voice of God or man

Depending on which voice you hear
Determines the direction your life will go
Satan is attacking people from all sides
Yes he is surrounding you each day

Anytime you step out for Christ
Satan's voice will approach you
His voice will speak to you
Christ is not the voice to hear

Satan speaks to us, to shame us saying
God doesn't know what's best for your life
God wants you to miss the good life
Which I can give to you

Don't let people tell you
There's not pleasure in worldly things
Yes there is pleasure for a while
But then it will come to an end

Satan doesn't show you the whole picture
He only shows you the best part of it
He knows if he would show you all
He could never get people to follow him

Like there is pleasure in drinking beer
It gives you a little buzz
Which makes you feel real good
So the next day you stop for another

Now you start stopping every day
Some days you even get drunk
You never know if you'll be the one
That will become an alcoholic

Then later down the road in life
You're so addicted to it
And you get cirrhosis of the liver
Then finally you take your last breath

But in the process of all of that
You lost your family and many friends
That tried to help you along the way
You said, having a drink would never hurt me

You drove down the road while drunk
Destroying the life of an innocent person
It didn't seem to bother you
For the bottle had control of you

The same goes with drugs
You think you can handle the first joint
And yes it makes you feel so good
You depend on it each and every day

Then someone came to you
Convincing you they have something better
So they give you a pill to try
Telling you it won't cost you a dime

But what they failed to tell you
Once you come down from that high
You now have to have another
Yet it cost you a lot of money

Before long it cost you too much
You don't have the money to buy
So they teach you how to steal
Just to get the fix your body needs

You've stolen everything from your family
You're now stealing from stores and others
Satan didn't tell you what would happen
When you smoked that first joint

Now you end up in jail
Time and time again
Then finally you shot someone
All because you needed that pill

You're now put in jail for life
You just don't love that jail time
But if you hadn't taken that first joint
You wouldn't be where you now are

Let me talk about another high
That is greater than them all
Which most people are overlooking
For they want to live their own life

That's a high on Jesus Christ
Which died for you and me
If you surrender All to Christ
And turn from the ways of your past

Seeking all he has for your life
Never to take your eyes off the goal
Seeking more of Christ every day
To please Christ in all you do

He'll take you to places you've never been
Excitement will well up in you
He'll give you a peace inside you
The more you desire Christ, he'll bless you

He'll show you how blessings will flow
By giving out of a heart of love
Not just talking about money
Which he commands us to give back

But when we share in the lives of others
After we weekly pay our tithes
You'll be so showered with blessings
You can't praise the Lord enough for them

God tells us in his Holy Word
If we will freely give
That we will also be blessed
Yes we can freely receive

When you hungry enough
He'll fill you with his Holy Spirit
Which will take you to higher heights
With the evidence of speaking in tongues

Think of all the gifts he has for us
We can receive every one we desire
But we must be willing to use them
To up lift the Lord, and no one else

Never stop at where you are today
There are always higher heights to climb
Christ wants you to be a happy person
As you live each day with Him

Anyone who tells you, you've reached the goal
That there's no place for you to go
Just turn around and smile at them
Telling them, God's not finished with me yet

Determine to live for Christ every day
Working for Christ, till you take your last breath
Be assured stumbling blocks will come your way
But don't let them determine if you're finished

Keep working for Christ every day
Even if you are flat on your back
There is always something for you to do
Even if it's sharing a kind word

So never give up on the Savior
Keep intact with him every day
Then the banquet table, will be prepared for you
You'll be so happy you didn't give up

Written On: 3-19-14

WHAT ABOUT THE SABAOTH DAY

Many people in the world
Try and stretch the Word to please themselves
For they don't want to follow
The instructions in God's word

God's word is so powerful
He knows what's best for us
So He wrote it in God's Word
To protect our lives on earth

We try to pick and choose what we want
For we think we know what's best
Then we end up twisting it
To meet our desires in life

People will hide what they are doing
By trying to bring up another subject
So you will be distracted
People won't realize what you're doing

The Sabbath day was given to us
So our bodies could rest from the week
For our bodies were worked hard
God knew our bodies would need rest

He told us in the scriptures
That as a child of God
We need to allow our bodies to rest
And our mind to be fed from God's word

That's why he placed the church in order
So our bodies could relax
As we bath in God's presence
Rather than forgetting who God is

You see all during the week
Our minds are focus on things to meet our needs
But Sunday was set aside
To get us focused back on Him

So we can realize God is our provider
He asks us to bring a tenth into the store house
Not just our money but also
Our time and our talents

Many bring their tithes to church
But they fail to worship the Lord
They are at church in body
Yet the Lord's far from their mind

All the time they're at church
There thinking about all the things
They will do after church
Forgetting, it is God's Holy day

Not realizing they can be blessed
If their heart is filled with God's love
Giving Him their whole heart
And not just a corner of the Sabbath day

They can get so much more accomplished
If they allow Christ to lead the way
For He knew the body needed rest
On the Sabbath day

So we defy the word of God
By working that extra day
Because the day brings more to our pocket
Then if we refused to work that day

We so often mow the lawn
And we work around the house
Defying God's Holy Word
When it was set aside for rest

We then wonder why we have many problems
In our lives day after day
Things like health problems, and break downs
You'll pay your tithes one way or another

The problem with paying it other ways
Rather than the principles in God's word
Is they won't benefit you
You'll be the one that loses

It could even keep you out of Heaven
Oh how sad that would be
For you could have used the Sabbath day
To keep your life intact

No, you defy the word of God
And drift too far from Christ
And then your life is snatched from you
An you end up in Hell

All because you defied God's Holy Word
Serving your life for self
You served that god self
Rather than serve the God of Heaven

So think about the Sabbath day
How do you use it each week?
Is the day, used giving the Lord
Your undivided attention?

Or has the Sabbath day become a ritual
And you come to church, to please your mind
And use the rest of the day
To serve self, rather than God

God won't make up your mind for you
He's given you a choice to make
Are you going to serve the God of Heaven?
Or is you mind set to serve self?

Written On: 12-1-11

WE CAN'T PLAY THE BLAME GAME

Blame seems to be the way of life
No matter where you turn
People love to point fingers
Without feeling bad about it

Adam and Eve in the garden
Were told not to eat from the tree of life
Once they both had taken part of it
They blamed it on the serpent

We forget that God gave to each
A will to do what we want
So whatever we do in life
We can't blame it on anyone but ourself

How often every day in life
We see people playing the blame game
They don't care in whom they hurt
As long as things turn out alright for them

We see children play this game every day
It happens on the playground at school
One child tells a lie on another
Your mind starts churning real fast

You can't accept the lie they told about you
So you punch them in the eye
Now they'll have a black eye
The teacher took their word rather than yours

The child that was hurt, blamed you
Saying you were the one that punched first
The blaming starts going back and forth
You shouldn't have punched that child

There are other ways to solve your problems
There is another means called love
Love will solve a multitude of sins
Without you raising a hand

We as parents are at the basis of it
For we fail to set the example
We tell our children to do certain things
But we live the opposite before them

We constantly blame our spouse
For things we've done before our children
So our children learn by our examples
To follow in our footsteps

If we would only live our lives well
Before our children in which we raise
When we make mistakes, be willing to repent
So our children know we are not perfect

How often do we hear these words
Do as I say, not as I do?
When you speak these type words
You're already setting your child up for a fall

Our teenagers are a reflection of us
We're not a person which showed real love
Too often a parent will say the right things
Yet they say it in a voice of hate

The teenager will not receive it
For you were unkind in how you spoke
So they quickly put up a fence
Between you as a youth, and mom and dad

We as parents argue about what goes on
With our boss we have at work
Then fire so often comes from our lips
Then we wonder why our children go wrong

This blaming goes on, down through life
Once this has taken control of you
It is nothing more than an attack of Satan
His desire is to destroy your life

All too often it's carried into the church
You have a chip on your shoulder
So you say things about God's servant
The Bible says we're not to come against them

We don't like the way he preaches
For conviction comes to our life
For my life doesn't measure up to the Bible
You love the life in which you live

But the things in which you're doing
Will keep you out of the portals of Heaven
So you as a servant of the Lord
Stop preaching the whole counsel of God

You think the Bible is out of date
You fail to realize it's a living book
Which means that it is up to date
No matter when in life you read it

Blaming is never a good thing
No matter how you look at it
You think blaming will get you somewhere
Yet it gives you a setback in your life

For it will eventually come back to haunt you
Then it will make you feel worse
If you had only told the truth
In a gentle voice so kindly

So why not strike the blame game
From the life in which you live
Your vocabulary will be more pleasant
And it will be pleasant to the Lord

Written On: 1-19-14

BEAUTY

How many times through life
Have you said these words?
"I wish that I was beautiful
Which everyone would love me so"

Many in the world today
Spend much time with a plastic surgeon
Planning out their next move
To make them look more beautiful

Surgery's don't really help them
For beauty doesn't come from the outside
Beauty starts down deep inside
The heart and soul of a person

Man will tell you you're not beautiful
For all they're looking at is your skin
You may not be beautiful in man's eyes
But you're the most beautiful in the eyes of God

What can make the ugliest person
Look beautiful to man and God
It's the joy that flows from the heart
Because Jesus lives inside them

You can be really over weight
Or too thin, you have no meat on your bones
You may have had an accident
And your face is full of scares

You see many are not satisfied
No matter what state they're in
Many have been cursed by Satan
That you'll never be satisfied

A beautiful person is always satisfied
With whatever state they find themselves in
They rejoice when things are going wrong
And rejoice when everything is alright

It's because they rejoice that one day
They will spend eternity with the Lord
For they rejoice where they'll finally be
In the presence of our Savior and Lord

They think about the Savior
When storms come to their lives
Knowing that whatever happens to the body
Will only last for a little while

Joy boils over from their soul
Because Jesus is number one in their life
Their only desire is to touch some soul
That they to, may have peace in their soul

Yes, the most beautiful people on earth
That are beautiful in man's eyes
Are the most unhappy people
For they don't have peace inside

Satan has planted in their mind
That they always must search for more
So they're never satisfied in their life
They're always searching for more

Won't you surrender all to Jesus
So you can be happy in whatever state you're in?
The things you face in this world
Won't overcome the joy of your soul

Living with heaven in your focus
Will help you have joy in your heart
So stop focusing on the current circumstances
Just keep focused on the Lord

Written On: 7-25-15

AS WE MOVE INTO FALL

Fall is now upon us
Time is rapidly passing along
It's seems as each season gets here
We then turn and it is gone

God has given each season to us
So we can enjoy what they provide
Each season has its own beauty
Let's look around and enjoy each of them

Winter, Summer, Spring, and Fall
They are all unique in their own way
Don't allow the seasons to pass you by
Without enjoying what they provide

Then remember who created them
Yes, God above gave us their beauty
For He wanted us to enjoy each one
To the fullest without complaining

Just think of the season which is about to arrive
Fall seems to be my favorite one
As the trees begin to turn colors
They're all types of shades and colors

Each type of tree has its own color
In which its beauty will spring forth
Not all turn at the same time
Just think how unique God is

The first one, which start turning
Are the soft wood trees out there
Maples, Popular, and so many more
Then their followed by the hardwood trees

Oaks, Hickey, and the Locust
We just look forward to seeing them all
They make you feel real good inside
As we take time to enjoy each one

Then you look across the broad fields
As the goldenrod start blooming
And all the flowers around the house
Take on brighter colors before the first frost

The dew is oh so heavy
Your feet get wet on the grass
And have you taken notice
The days are rapidly getting shorter

Men are out picking apples
And digging the potatoes to stash away
For those winter months ahead
So we have food to eat during the winter

We think of fall as harvest time
A wonderful time for hay rides
A time to bob for apples
It's a fun time all around

Just think of God our provider
He gives us all of these good things
Won't you take time to enjoy them?
God wants to bring joy to every one

Just look around at the fall decorations
Many people have been inspired
Just learn to enjoy all of God's beauty
As each one is only here for a little while

Written On: 9-20-15

"WANT TO BE"

People in the world today
Tell you what they "want to be"
But "want to be" controls their life
And nothing changes for them

They live their life everyday
Never planning anything out
Bless God they would never set a goal
For they think it will control there life

So each day in which they live
They want to accomplish many things
They won't allow planning to control their life
So they don't accomplish anything

I lived this way all my life
Don't try and change the way I live
For this is the way I've always lived
And bless God don't try and change me

The thinking in which they have
They will accomplish little or nothing
You will always see them sitting around
Pondering all the things they "want to be"

Not realizing setting goals for their life
Will bring freedom not bondage to them
They don't realize the attitude which they have
Will have them in bondage all of their life

If you find yourself in that situation
You can be freed from it my friend
But you must get rid of "want to be"
And get clothed in I will, for my life

It will change the state you've been in
If you'll walk with the Lord each day
If you'll keep focused on the Savior
Instead of who, I "want to be"

Christ has a plan for each of us
If we seek the Lord to find his will
His will, will lead you down the right path
To the place of peace and rest

If you have the mentality most people have
You'll always live in bondage my friend
For that is Satan speaking through you
Self is controlling your life

There's safety in numbers
If you surround yourself with believers
Which will help to lift you up each day
Rather than pull yourself down

Too many have that mentality
I want to be separated to myself
So the "want to be" is controlling you
The hole in your heart is getting bigger

That's exactly where Satan wants you
Now he has control of your life
Then you can't see where you are
For the "want to be" has control of you

Oh you go to the church, when the doors are open
You read and pray every day
But you're not advancing in the life you live
You want to control God, so you're living for self

You're always telling God what you will do
It's your will rather than the Lord's
So the circumstances you find yourself in
Are not pleasing to the Lord

Satan has you believing my friend
That you're on the right path
But that path is leading to destruction
Without you realizing where you are

You're headed to a devils Hell
I'm talking about believers in the Lord
For you're always wanting what you desire
Rather than the will of God for your life

You think you have it all together
Yet you're miserable down inside
Saying bless God that's how I'll do it
Rather than except God's will for my life

Oh yes you search the scriptures
For the things you want to hear
To prove that you are right
And everyone else I meet is wrong

You'll turn away good counsel
For bless God I know what's right
Even if I live a life of misery
I know what's best for me

What others say about my life
I'll not let them bother me
I know what's best in my life
I'll not yield to what I hear

But most of the things that you hear
Is a reflection of your own life
The mentality which you're carrying
Is deeply embedded in your heart

So I'll keep living the way I want
And not to take counsel from others
I'll surround myself with weak believers
For I can mold them into my will for them

If you find yourself with this attitude
You're setting yourself up for a fall
God will only allow you to go so far
He'll then pull the rug from under you

Then you'll find yourself empty
Wondering how you ended there
For some it may be too late
An now you blame it on the Lord

You see God is a loving God
He'll take you as high as you want to go
But when you start taking the praise
He'll take you down to the lows

Do you think you have it all together?
Be assured you have much to learn
If you're not setting aside your desires
Seeking what God wants for your life

Saying to the Lord, "this is the way I see it
But is there something that I'm missing
That may be leading me down the wrong path
Where you could eventually cut me off

I want all you have for me
Not my will but thine be done
If there's anything I need to change
I want to change as you speak to me

I know you speak in many ways
It could be while reading the Word
It could be while I'm in prayer with you
But be assured I want your will

He could send a believer in my path
Help me be attentive to listen to them
Rather than to be the dominate person
For I don't have time to hear them out

So Lord I yield myself to you
Not my will but thine be done
And as you reveal things to me
I'll be willing to change to please you"

Written On: 7-3-14

UP SIZING

Up sizing is so very enticing
We seem to love it today
Up sizing seems to puff us up
But is it good, or is it bad

Let's take a look at it
Yes, analyze this strange thing
But when you take a look at it
You'll understand it much better

We love going to fast food restaurants
We see all the menus on the wall
We take a good look at them
We decide we're hungry for one of them

You tell the one behind the counter
You want the meal number three
Then the cashier speaks this to you
Do you want to up size your meal

Now you have a choice to make
Will I gorge myself or not
For it only cost a quarter
In order to get a lot more

So you tell them to go ahead
And up size the meal you've chosen
You take the meal to your table
You seem to enjoy eating all that meal

You get up from the table
It strikes you right away
You have eaten too much food
Now you feel miserable as you leave

But you keep going back each day
Up sizing each meal you purchase
You start gaining so much weight
You don't understand that it is a sin

That's the bad thing about up sizing
You feel miserable every day
Now you can't do your work properly
You have gained too much weight

Now that we've seen that it was a bad thing
Could it be a good thing for you?
If we had only used it properly
It wouldn't have become a sin at all

If you had only bought that meal.
An up sized it for you and your wife
Sharing all those fry's and drink
You wouldn't have gained all that weight

The extra would have been a good thing
You wouldn't have gorged yourself
And shared what you bought with others
And you'd have saved money in the process

How about when you go out and buy a car
So many buy a very small one
The purpose of that small car
Is to make you feel real good

It is a very bright red
And a two door car you see
You think it will make you feel good
So you buy the car for yourself

You drive the car home
To show your wife and kids
You had traded in the family car
You made the family oh so mad

They wanted to go for a drive
He could only take one at a time
They knew when they went to the grocery store
There wasn't room to bring them all home

You don't have another car
And no money to buy another one
How foolish a person you were
A man that just lived for self

What if you had bought a four door car[;
For you, your wife, and two kids
And you had room for two more people
Which you could have invited to church

There is another up sizing
Which should be the most important to your life
That is up grading the life that you live
Serving Christ with all your heart

Yes you have accepted Christ into your life
And you go to church every week
Giving Christ one or two hours each week
Which helps you feel real good

But God wants to speak to your heart
He wants you to surrender all to him
Then when you give Him your total life
You'll then up size to greater things

He'll bless you in ways you may not know
You say it's impossible to achieve
But when God is behind everything you do
Impossible things can happen to you

We hear of very few things happening
Out in the world in which we live
For we are ashamed to take the gospel
Out of the four walls of the church

God didn't give us the gospel to hold to ourself
So we're the only one that hears the truth
But he wants us to go out into the world
And tell others that Jesus still lives

It's when we take the gospel to others
It will make an impact you see
Into the hearts and lives of others
So others will be saved from Hell

You never know what it will do for you
It will up size you to greater things
Yes your life will be totally blessed
So you can be a greater blessing for Christ

You see serving Jesus is not for ourselves
But so we can shine for Him
So stop living for yourself every day
And make Christ number one in your life

It is then that rewards will start coming to you
All he asks for is our obedience
Won't you get started this very day
And let Christ rule and reign in your life?

It's when we make our goal Heaven
And live each day for it
There is a place in Heaven for us
And will be welcomed in my friend

But if you keep fooling around
With your eyes taken off the goal
The light of Heaven will go out
And the only destination will be Hell

Written On: 3-23-14

TRUTH OR UNTRUTH

Truth or untruth, what are you seeking?
Most will tell you they want truth
But how you treat the subject
May tell otherwise

Because of how people treat God's Word
Our churches are filled with untruth
That's why so many which sit in the pew
Their minds are filled with untruth

You may ask how can you say that?
It happens in all churches
Which we think are preaching God's Word
But digging deep you find untruth.

We've been blinded from the whole truth
Because we approach God's Word the wrong way
And our way leads to half truth
Yet we deal with it as truth

This is how most approach God's Word
They find scriptures to prove they are right
And never deal with the other half truth
Which defies your truth

How can you know how to find
The truth in God's Holy Word
Stop trying to find how to prove you are right
But start proving God's Word is right

If we only try proving we are right
We never see the opposite in God's word
What we must always remember is
There are hidden things in God's Holy book

That's why God's Word is a living book
He will speak to people who are hungry
He hides things in His Holy Word
To keep us from being lazy

If he laid everything out plain for us
We would only become more relaxed
In our walk with the Lord each day
And we would fail to follow God's word

It has been proven that man advances most
When persecution comes their way
When persecution ceases in our life
We tend to sit back and relax

When Christians win a battle
The first thing they do is
Feel satisfied they have won
Then they sit back until the next problem comes

But those of the world work differently
They never miss a beat when they lose
They just keep using other tactics
Which may be hidden from us

Always remember Satan is a deceiver
It's time we take back the ground we've lost
Quit relaxing in our walk with Christ
Until we as believers take our last breath

There's no time in a Christian's life
To retire when we get old
We may not be able to do what we once did
Yet we can change to a different roll

Our manual labor may be over
Yet there's so much we can do
We learn it from God's Holy Word
By digesting it every day

By leaning on the Holy Spirit
To guide us each step we take
That's how we'll know we're in God's will
Rather than following what we desire

When we don't take on the mind of Christ
Embracing what He desires for our life
And only what we want to believe
We'll not be in the will of God

That's why we get caught up in wacky things
Which are only half truths
And we lead many people astray
We've not taken on the mind of Christ

You may say what are you talking about?
This subject has plagued my mind for so long
I was torn from both sides
Not understanding why God's Word was two faced

You see it was only in these last few years
That I really got serious before the Lord
And I started understanding what God
Requires of a believer in His Word

My insides were being torn apart
By people which believed the opposite
And they could prove their point you see
By God's Word it made me so disturbed

That subject is <u>Once Saved Always Saved</u>
I've found it to be a very dangerous teaching
You who believe that teaching
Please take time to hear me out

Both sides of this subject
Could give me scriptures in God's Word
Which could convince others
That there teaching was the truth

Yet each failed to fill in the gap
How they believed on each side
So when you see the argument each makes
It made my God a liar

Or could it be we're missing something
Which each side uses to prove their point
And looking at the side each takes
Proves they're right and the other is wrong

Yet God's word never lies, my friend
If it did, God wouldn't be God
So I took the stand, God can't lie
Finally my eyes were opened to see

From the very beginning of time
God gave each of us a will
Remember we must interpret scripture with scripture
If we don't, we interpret it wrong

So I finally took the attitude
Lord no matter which way I believe
Will you show to me
What I'm missing in your word

No matter which way I believe
It's not important that I get my way
But that your truth, falls from my lips
And all my thinking needs cast away

That's when my thoughts took on a new meaning
And as I read God's word each day
I'm looking for God's will
Rather than allow my will to dominate

Now knowing God gave us all a will
That started gears in my brain
How could God give us a will
Then force us, to stay in his will

Then it started opening my mind
To process so much more
The scripture which says, in John 10:28
No man can pluck you out

Now after reading it many times
I said Lord, now you have a problem
For this scripture clashes with other scripture
Which makes me more confused

I went to bed, thinking on this one night
Saying Lord, How can you settle my mind?
For I am more confused than ever
As I put these two passages together

It plagued me most of the night
Little sleep came to my eyes
For I desired God's will
The Holy Spirit was planting food in my soul

He spoke unto my spirit saying again
Read that passage one more time
Yes, know man can pluck you out
Of your life my precious friend

It hit me like a bolt of lightning falling from the sky
Yes, no man can pluck you out
But, your daily choices
Of our God given will, can

I then drifted off to sleep
A peaceful rest, the remainder of the night
The Lord put a principle in me
Which I will never forget

The next day I wrote it all down
What the Holy Spirit revealed to me
And He planted it in my heart
So I could share it with all I see

But God wasn't through with me yet
The thought of the scripture, many quoted to me
Ephesian 4:30, rang so clearly in my ear
You are sealed, till the day of redemption

Once again this verse pledged my soul
But the Holy Spirit spoke to me
If you are serious before the Lord
I'll open your mind, unto my word

He placed a thought in my mind
Which I never want to forget
It answered the question put before me
That you're sealed, until your life ends

Whether it be through our death
Or the rapture of God takes place
Yes on God's part, He seals it
Yet we, as an individual, can break it

He placed in my mind a story
I will never forget my friend
For it settled the question in my mind
Can a seal ever be broken?

A story of a truck driver
Picked up a load on the west coast
The company placed a seal on it
To not be broken till it reached the east coast

Halfway through the trip east
The driver got curious, to what he was hauling
Could it be drugs, or something else
Which could get him in trouble

He found a secluded, pullover place
Broke the seal, and inspected the load
This is how Satan works on believers
Places doubts down deep in our soul

And if we don't cut him off right away
By repenting of those sins we have
They will keep piling up
Until the seal of our heart is broken

But the driver didn't stop there
He found glue to seal it back
But it left a mark, on the seal
Which was detected, when he reached the east coast

Yes God's seal is placed upon you
Once you accept Christ into your heart
But it's up to us, to keep it intact
By staying close to the cross

We can waver too many times
Without repenting, for the wrongs we've done
Not God, but we can break the seal
By not keeping clean, our live from sin

We many times will do things
Knowing God's not pleased with it
That's when we live, close to the edge
A place no Christians, should ever live

Yes, if we stay there too long
We'll break the seal, Christ places on us
That's a bad place to be found
For many will lose their salvation

Many say if you're in that place
You never accepted Christ, into your life
And for many you are truly right
Yet for some, they were born again

They served the Lord for many years
Yet they left their guard down too many times
And Satan kept tempting them
You stayed, too close to the edge

And finally Satan wins out
You spent, less and less time in prayer
The world crowds out bible study
You start pleasing man, instead of the Lord

If you hadn't started compromising
The principles in God's Holy Word
Pushing the Holy Spirit aside
Your desires to please man, would not have taken over

Satan's time is running out
Then the Lord's time will begin
When He'll remove sickness and pain
And all troubles, Satan brings our way

Many problems you face in life today
God allows them to come your way
Not to punish you, but help you grow
Much stronger in the Lord

Stop blaming your trials upon the Lord
But keep focused on the King of Kings
Knowing your trials are only for a season
You'll come out stronger on the other side

Always remember this life we live on earth
Is a training ground, to prepare us for Heaven
This life which we live here on earth
Will determine where we will spend eternity

The trials we face upon this earth
Compared to the hereafter
Eternity never ends my friend
Where will you, spend it

The Lord is keeping records
Satan has no reasons for records you see
Satan only wants as many as he can
Those he can deceive, right into Hell

He doesn't care if your life is filled
With good things upon this earth
As long as they consume the time
You should be spending with the Lord

Consuming the time you should be praying
Seeking the Lord's will for your life
And the time you should be spending each day
Telling others about the Lord Jesus Christ

No! Satan only has one purpose
To deceive you into the pit of Hell
So you'll be tormented along with him
He doesn't want you to know, you can avoid it

But God has your best at heart
He truly wants you to live with Him
But He gives you a choice to make
Will you live for Christ or be deceived into Hell

The good thing about being a Christian
He reigns both on the just an unjust
But the just He'll walk beside you
Through the trials you face in this life

He doesn't separate you from the world
For he wants us to be a light
In this dark world, in which we live
So others may be drawn to Christ

You may be the only one they see
Is your light burning bright or dim?
You have a choice of how you'll live
Don't let your light burn out

That's why the <u>once saved always saved</u> teaching
Is so dangerous to those who embrace it
It gives them room to sin in their lives
Thinking they'll still end up in Heaven

The other thing I see in it
Others believe they can say the sinner's prayer
Then leave the alter just as they came
And Heaven is awaiting them

You may say that cannot be
And in your mind your thinking right
But the one which just prayed the sinners pray
Leaves believing that they will make it to Heaven

Remember you told them they were saved
When they left that alter of prayer
Yet you didn't know if they meant it or not
You have deceived them right into Hell

The greatest advice I'll give to you
Is live each day as if it were your last
After you have surrendered your life
To the Lord Jesus Christ

If you live this way you'll make
An impact wherever you go
And you'll be surprised when you get to Heaven
All the souls you will see up there

The ones God will show you
That you watered and planted on earth
Yes, I'm looking at multitudes of souls
That made it to heaven for my obedience to Christ

Souls that will be your souls
Are yours in two different ways
Some will be for pointing them to Christ
And living their life to light up this world

Yet another great way to win souls
Is through our giving of what God blesses us with
Supporting missionaries, ministries and the local church
The souls they reach are also yours

So if you are one that has a hard time
Speaking into the lives of others
Find missionaries and ministries that uplift Christ
Giving to them through a heart of love

Then don't fail to lift them up in prayer
The souls they will reach every day
Yes those souls which they reach
Are also souls which you have reached

You may say how can that be?
They can reach the multitudes my friend
With the support of people like you
Which are willing to pray and give

So you see, God has a work for each of us
Pray for God's will for your life
Then watch for the opportunity
Then step through the door God opens

The door may not be comfortable at first
But be assured, God will lead you along
If you will become faithful
To the task God sets before you